A Life With Wings

by
Marge Green

*"They that wait for Jehovah shall renew their strength;
they shall mount up with wings as eagles; they shall
run, and not be weary; they shall walk, and not faint."*
Isaiah 40:31

ISBN   0-89137-402-7 (paper),
0-89137-403-5 (cloth).

Published by

 **QUALITY PUBLICATIONS**
P.O. Box 1060   Abilene, Texas 79604

This work is dedicated to
DEL GREEN
who loves me when I am unlovable;
lends me strength when I am weak;
and exemplifies all I try to teach.

HIGH FLIGHT

Oh! I have slipped the surly bonds of earth
    And danced the skies on laughter-silvered wings;
Sunward I've climbed, and joined the tumbling mirth
    Of sun-split clouds—and done a hundred things
You have not dreamed of—wheeled and soared and swung
    High in the sunlit silence. Hov'ring there
I've chased the shouting wind along, and flung
    My eager craft thro' footless halls of air.

Up, up the long, delirious, burning blue
I've topped the wind-swept heights with easy grace
Where never lark, nor even eagle flew—
    And while with silent, lifting mind I've trod
The high, untrespassed sanctity of space,
    Reached out my hand and touched the face of God.

                John Gillespie Magee
                born 1922, killed in air combat 1941
Used through kindness of the United States Air Force Recruiting Service.

CREDIT WHERE CREDIT IS DUE

In any work of this nature, it would be virtually impossible to be absolutely original in every thought and word. I certainly do not claim any such perfection in this little book. I have gleaned much good from many sources. I have tried to give proper credit in every instance where I have used words of another and even if I have only borrowed a seed of a thought. In some cases I have used ideas of others in developing a fuller writing and have tried to give credit for these also.

I am desirous of giving special credit where this credit is due. It is not my wish to claim as my own, another's work and without the list which follows, I would have had a much more difficult time in producing this work. I give my heartfelt appreciation and sincere "Thank You"—

To the Air Force who gave me permission to use the poem in the front of this book. This poem is used in a television commercial from the United States Air Force and expresses its thought beautifully.

To Hannah Whitall Smith and her **The Christian's Secret of Happiness.**
To Elton Trueblood and His **Company of the Committed.**
To Howard Whitman and his **"The American Way of Love."**
To an unknown author whose ten evaluation questions in Chapter II were given during an inspirational radio program. The station did not have the name of this person when I sought it.

To Sister Henry Speck and her lectures at the 1965 ACC Lectureship. I took many notes and spoke with Sister Speck afterwards, telling her I intended to use some of her thoughts in my future teaching. She was most gracious, saying they were not all original with her. I also heard her speak at a ladies' luncheon several years ago on "Don't Quit—Qualify." Some thoughts from this speech have been used also. Her talks were of much help in developing the chapters on mental health and personal responsibility.

To Mrs. R. E. B. Fielder of Van Alstine, Texas, who wrote the poem "A Plea for Tolerance" which appears in Chapter III. A copy of this work was given me by my aunt, Mrs. J. W. Bass. An effort to reach Mrs. Fielder personally has met with failure. Mail has been returned but I am including her lovely poem since it so adequately expresses the thoughts of tolerance. I pray she will accept my thanks in this way.

To Brother Joe West who enabled me to tour Abbott Laboratories in Waukegan, Illinois. It was this tour which inspired me to write Chapter IV.

To J. B. Phillips' **Your God Is Too Small.** It was from this work that Chapter V was developed. The views of God used are Mr. Phillips'. I have adapted them to fit my lesson.

To Sister Addie Gililland, a very able teacher of God's word. The chapter on the tongue was developed from a lesson she gave while I served as her assistant during a vacation Bible school at the Highland Church of Christ in Abilene, Texas.

To Brother Stafford North and his wonderful tract, "Learning the Fine Art of Worship." This little booklet helped me in preparing the chapter on "Audience Participation." Sister Linda Haedge also gave me much help with this chapter from the notes she took at the York College Lectureship, 1965.

To Robert Boyd Munger's tract, "My Heart—Christ's Home." This small leaflet was purchased at an Evangelical Church store after being recommended by Sister Nell Hall, who had used its idea for a visual aid for her Bible class.

Some of my benefactors must of necessity remain unnamed for I have no way of knowing who they are. Nevertheless to those "Anonymous" ones I add my thanks too. Perhaps they will know who they are.

If this list is incomplete, I ask forgiveness. I have tried faithfully to give credit where credit is due and pray that I have done so.

TABLE OF CONTENTS

FOREWORD

The day had been long and tiring. As the afternoon wore into evening I went out on the back patio and sat down for a brief rest. The tensions of my mind and the weariness of my body began to ease and I relaxed, looking out over the lake. All was quiet except for the faint hum of traffic from the freeway not too far away. Suddenly my attention was caught by a small group of birds, wheeling and dipping over the water. I began watching them. They seemed so contented, so happy, up there in the sky. With casual carefulness they would sweep down and pick up some insect from the surface of the lake and then with great confidence once again soar up toward the heavens.

How wonderful it would be if we human beings could know such ease of movement and complete contentment in life! Surely all that could harm those birds down on earth must seem so small from their vantage point high above. With little effort they could leave those dangers and sweep upward to safety. The miracle of flight was truly God's gift to these, His creatures of beauty.

Later, when I came back to the routine of my life, my mind kept going back to those birds. Somewhere I knew there was a parallel drawn from their example and I thought it was in the Old Testament. I got out my concordance and began to search. There were many references to the birds of the air but I finally found the one for which I was looking. Isaiah 40:31!

"They that wait for Jehovah shall renew their strength; they shall mount up with wings as eagles; they shall run, and not be weary; they shall walk, and not faint."

Here was what I would write of next! I knew the title of my new book. No clearer parallel could be drawn than that of the flight of the eagle and the triumphant Christian life which was promised to each of us when our Savior said, "I came that they may have life, and may have it more **abundantly**" (John 10:10). This abundant life and a life with wings must be one and the same! And now my task lay before me. Could I make these thoughts come alive on paper? Would the readers see this parallel as clearly as I? I knew that I must at least try and with God's help and His will directing me, I would not fail. The following pages are the result of this pledge and were written with the prayerful earnest desire that every person who will read these words might catch a realistic glimpse of what the Christian life was meant to be. And I pray that we might pull ourselves away from the "legalistic" duty-bound existence which most have made of their life in Christ. I state now that a life in Christ is not—repeat, NOT—the semi-misery which seems to characterize so many Christians. I can positively tell you (because God's word tells **me**) that the life committed to the Savior cannot help but be contented, joyous and fruitful beyond all our expectations! If you cannot believe this, the further pages of this book will be of little, if any, use to you. But if you do believe this and have the courage to step with me beyond the bounds of this weary old earth, maybe together we can soar with the wings promised us by that prophet of old.

Flight has always signified freedom to man. Ancient historians and writers of mythology tell us of man's desire to loose the bounds of earth and soar above to the heights of the sky. His first attempts were feeble indeed but as time passed, man began to find ways to lift his body into the air. Now, in the Twentieth Century, we have come so far that a human being has walked in space! And the dreams of humanity continue ever upward to unheard of and unscaled heights.

But even with the ability to take his physical body up beyond the earth and into the void of space, man's spiritual being still remains rooted to its earthly environs. He possesses enough knowledge to lift great weight from the planet he lives on but for some reason, mankind generally has missed the truth whereby he can cause his soul to be carried far above the cares and troubles which so tormentingly anchor it to the world. God gave man the necessary mental capacity with which he can search out the secrets of sending people into space. But more important, our Creator also gave man the formula whereby he can make his daily life one of great peace, joy and freedom. If we go to such pains to put ourselves on the moon, should we not put forth **some** effort to elevate our existence here on earth to a level which will not only bring happiness now, but carries with it the promise of eternal bliss in the presence of God and our Savior, Jesus Christ?

In traveling around this great nation of ours and speaking with groups of Christian women, I see a deep yearning to have this life which allows one to move calmly through the storms which daily sweep over us. The world is moving fast and each day brings new problems. Sorrows come to all; tragedy seems to seek us out. Is this what the Christian life is supposed to be? Did God send Christ to this earth merely to save our souls in the judgment or was He interested in what happens to us here and now? So many Christians wallow in the misery of too much **negative** Truth, while seeming to ignore the far more prevalent and exalting **positive** Truth. It is this attitude which keeps us from enjoying the abundant life promised us by Christ.

I can say with all certainty that God **does** care about our life now; He is interested in what happens to us. His word is full of positive principles which will enrich our lives and cause us truly to believe Philippians 4:6, 7.

"In nothing be anxious; but in everything by prayer and supplication with thanksgiving let your requests be made known unto God. And the peace of God, which passeth all understanding, shall guard your hearts and your thoughts in Christ Jesus."

But this life is not a half-way, half-hearted existence. No, it must be a whole-hearted, completely trusting commitment to God, His Son and their way for us. What He says, we must be willing to do—putting from our mind any doubt. If He gives a promise, we can be assured He will keep it. We must be busy, not concerning ourselves with what God will do, but with what **we** can do. He is a certainty; we can trust Him completely. It's the human element we can't trust and this is what this book is all about.

I shall try to be as practical as possible in every aspect of this life I am urging you to try. I will give the Bible principles, but I will also attempt to put this into living action. For until we, as Christians, can take the word of Truth and make it a daily walk of life, we are merely repositories of a good theory. The best evidence of Christianity is the Christian life, not all the theological arguments I might present. So my purpose in writing this book is to give as many useful and achievable suggestions as possible.

I do not claim originality in all of these thoughts, for many people have enriched my life with their deeds, writing, lessons and sermons. I have gained much from other Christians and though I could not begin to name them all, I want to mention a few. Dwain Evans, w h o s e life exemplifies the total commitment which I am trying to write about. Sisters Nell Hall, Linda Haedge and Addie Gililland, who furnished ideas for some of the lessons. Sister T. B. Thompson. Sister Jo Bass. Sister Bea Speck's lessons at the 1965 ACC Lectureship. And all the women and girls in every class I've ever taught. I owe much to these and also many others whose names are written in my heart. The true credit for this work does not belong in my hands alone but to all those who have been a part of my life since I became a Christian in 1948.

And above all, I recognize that these pages could never have been produced without the help of God. Like Paul, I must say, "Not that we are sufficient of ourselves, to account anything as from ourselves; but our sufficiency is from God" (II Corinthians 3:5).

"A life with wings" is that Christian life which is lived out here on earth but centered in heaven. With this life we can soar far above all that hinders us from reaching upward to God. We can cope with any problem, face any sorrow, live with any grief if we just take to our "wings." From our high vantage point of spiritual flight, we can put all these fetters of life in their proper place. We can view them in the true perspective of the Christian's promise of the "peace that passeth all understanding." We can pass over and beyond them, drawing ever nearer to the presence of God.

Won't you take the first step necessary for this life by putting your life in the hand of Him who made you? Trust in His help, but be willing to take that first stride in His direction. Then, you can truly "loose the surly bonds of earth . . . and touch the face of God." Come, won't you at least try your wings?

SUGGESTED READING LIST

Gift from the Sea by Anne Morrow Lindbergh.
Pantheon Books, New York, New York.
Keepers of the Springs by Peter Marshall.
Fleming H. Revell Company, Westwood, New Jersey
The Prophet by Kahlil Gibran.
Alfred A. Knopf Publisher, New York, New York.
Your God Is Too Small by J. B. Phillips.
The Macmillan Company, New York, New York.
The Kingship of Self-Control by William George Jordan.
Fleming H. Revell Company, Westwood, New Jersey.
The Company of the Committed by Elton Trueblood.
Harper and Row Publishers, New York, New York.
The Christian's Secret of a Happy Life by Hannah Whitall Smith.
Fleming H. Revell Company, Westwood, New Jersey.
Try Giving Yourself Away by David Dunn.
Prentice-Hall, Inc., Englewood Cliffs, New Jersey.

CHAPTER I

"A TOTAL COMMITMENT"

"Have Thine own way, Lord, have Thine own way. Thou art the Potter; I am the clay. Mold me and make me, after Thy will. While I am waiting, yielded and still."

How many Christians sing this beautiful hymn without realizing the prayer they have just uttered? We lift our voices with the words but don't really intend for God to take us seriously. At least our everyday actions give evidence to that fact. We ask God to have His way with us, to mold us after His will. Then we struggle daily to accomplish the task by ourselves. Perhaps we could see the parallel better if we would imagine ourselves to be a lump of clay. We might desire to be a beautiful and functional piece of pottery but could we produce the desired results alone? Certainly not. There must be a potter willing to take us into his hands, molding and shaping, until we become what he has in mind for us.

Then why do we as Christians sing this song and not yield our lives to the Potter? Hannah Whitall Smith puts it this way, "Just as the potter, however skilful, cannot make a beautiful vessel out of a lump of clay that is never put into his hands, so neither can God make out of me a vessel unto His honor unless I put myself into His hands. And as God is **sure** to do His part all right, the vital thing for me is to find out what my part is, and then do it."

And my part is committing my life—totally and completely—to God! No doubts, no reservations, for God is faithful and just and never slack in His promises. He has promised an "abundant life," a "peace that passeth understanding," but He will not f o r c e us to let this life be ours. We must believe that He means what He says and with that faith, take the steps necessary to place our life in His hands to be molded and fashioned as He has willed. I am convinced too many Christians feel that after their baptism, God leaves them to their own devices to get through this earthly existence. Then on the day of judgment He will once again take the power over our life. But a study of His word does not support this idea. He has promised to be with us "always, even to the end of the world." Does this sound as though He is not interested in helping us here and now? In fact, a closer study of the Bible indicates that more instructions are given the Christian to help him attain the abundant life than those given to instruct him how to become a child of God. Surely this should tell us that He does care and that He is ever ready to work His will in us, if we have the faith to believe — **really** believe — what He says.

Total commitment sounds ominous, almost frightening. Yet it should not! The commitment of which I speak is a joyful process, relieving the heart of its guilt and bringing an unbelievable peace to the soul. Perhaps it is the "total" part about which we have reservations, thinking that this removes any responsibility on the human part. Take this thought from your mind right away, for this is not true. God did not create a mass of robots or puppets which He manipulates for His own pleasure. He endowed us with a mind and gave us the right to make our own choices. To commit our way to Him does not imply He takes up the "strings" of our life, moving us any way He chooses. Rather it is a blending of wills, submitting our human will to His divine will and together we move through life, each doing his part in this commitment.

A clearer understanding of the word **commitment** should help us discern the true meaning of what this life is all about. First, a commitment is an entrusting of something to another, in complete confidence that it will be cared for to the best of that person's ability. This is God's part. We give Him our lives, our all, to keep until the day of accounting. He will do just that. We can have confidence that "all things work together for good to those that love the Lord" and this means He is active in the oversight of our daily lives. His providential care covers us and we are secure in His keeping.

Second, a commitment is a pledging of one's energies, purposes and loyalty to a cause. This is **our** part. Once we commit our lives to God and know that it is safe in His hands, then we can diligently busy ourselves in furthering His cause. We need not waste our time in worry or concern over what is happening in the pattern of living — the problems, sorrows, tragedies. These are safely cared for by the one to whom we have committed them. Now our time and energies can be utilized in serving the purposes of the church, which is God's "cause" on earth. We now have the time to concern ourselves with others; teaching His way to the lost; finding new abilities to develop in His service.

So you can see that total commitment need not be frightening nor complex. God has His part and we have ours. We can be sure He will fulfill His end and this should give us great confidence so that we can keep ours. From the beginning God has known what is best for man and when erring humanity realizes this and has the faith to truly **believe** it, life can be peaceful, fruitful and joyful beyond any expectation. If we desire to lead the righteous life, the answer is in this total commitment to God.

"Commit thy way unto Jehovah; trust also in him and he will bring it to pass. And he will make **thy righteousness go forth as the light** and thy justice as the noonday. Rest in Jehovah and wait patiently for him" (Psalms 37:5-7).

How do we make this commitment? What are the ways we take to place ourselves in His hands? First, let me say that this is written primarily for those who have already made the first step in this direction. They have heard His word, believed that Jesus is the Son of God, confessed this fact and repented of their sins. Their baptism then placed them in the body of Christ and they are now children of God. To those who may not have taken this step, may I urge you to study God's word so that you might become a Christian. Until you are, God'cannot offer you the promises reserved for His own family. Being born into the family of God is the basic step which everyone must take in committing his life to the Father.

WE MUST COMMIT OUR PAST TO GOD. When we arise from the waters of baptism, we have in a very real sense given our past to God to take care of. And this He has the power and authority to do (Mark 2:7). He passed this authority to Christ (Matthew 9:6). And we can be assured He will be faithful in taking care of that past life of sin (I John 1:9). What does He do with the past life we commit to Him? It is blotted out, erased, completely forgiven and forgotten! "And their sins and iniquities will I remember no more" (Hebrews 10:17).

But what about the past which we are building up just in the passing of days after we become Christians? Is it committed to God also? With confidence I answer "Yes!" John, the apostle whom Christ loved, tells us if we confess our sins, "He is faithful and righteous to forgive us our sins, and to cleanse us from all unrighteousness" (I John 1:9). Certainly we will make mistakes, even in a committed life. We are human and the same passage in I John, verse 10 tells us that we all sin. But with our trust completely in Christ, we need have no fear that these transgressions will divert us from the righteous life. We simply take them to God through our mediator, Christ, and they are remembered no more. The past need cause no worry for us!

WE MUST COMMIT OUR PRESENT TO GOD. This is perhaps the hardest of all for us to do. We tend to hang on tenaciously, trying by the might of our own strength to meet the problems of daily life. We cannot do it victoriously! It is not within human nature to do all the things or to be all that we should. BUT it is within Christ's nature to take on all the hurdles of this life and move through them safely. How does this benefit the Christian? If we keep the commandments of God, then Christ dwells within us (I John 3:24). His nature and will are blended with ours and **then** we are able to accomplish the task of living in the chaos of the world without ourselves becoming chaotic. Christ, dwelling within us, causes us to live the abundant life in accordance with the will of our Father.

"I have been crucified with Christ; and it is no longer I that live, but Christ liveth in me: and that life which I now live in the flesh I live in faith, the faith which is in the Son of God, who loved me, and gave himself up for me" (Galatians 2:20). Paul knew that within himself he could accomplish nothing, but with Christ he could do all things. Certainly he had a part in this. He tells us he had to buffet his own body daily to bring it into subjection. Yet this buffeting was the battle to make his will blend with that of Christ. This was the daily committing which he had to do. But I have not said this life was one of ease. God did not promise this and of course, I could not say that Christianity is not work. It is simple, though, because God does not require of us that which is too hard to do. The difficult part comes in battling our own will in order to let God have His way.

WE MUST COMMIT OUR FUTURE TO GOD. It is not within the human realm to know what the future holds. Therefore very little we can do will assure that future to be safe and happy. The Christian does not concern himself with what might lie ahead. He commits the days before him to God and living in the present in a positive way, the coming years will be taken care of. Our heavenly Father has not guaranteed us a certain number of days here on earth. He simply tells us to take one day at a time, living it with His help. Since we can do so little to secure the future, it is only reasonable that we should rely completely upon God to see that all is well with us as we meet the days to come.

If we believe Romans 8:28, then the future can hold nothing which should alarm us. Christ has given us all things which pertain to life and godliness (I Peter 1:3) and He has also told us the requirements for a good life (I Peter 3:10, 11). The things we can do in the present to insure good days ahead, we must do with a willing heart. But in the final analysis, we must leave the future in God's hands and trust He will secure it for us.

WE MUST COMMIT OUR SALVATION TO GOD. It has always been the custom of man to devise enticing theories and practices whereby he seeks to please his Maker. But the wise man of the Old Testament recognized that human wisdom was just not adequate to direct his way. And if man does not have the ability to direct his own way here on earth, how could he begin to save himself for eternity? How foolish to entrust our salvation to anyone or any thing other than the Divine Being who created all we see and set it in order for our well-being!

Like some of the characters we read about in both secular and divine history, we set up gods to ourselves who cannot deliver us. Jezebel's prophets could not rouse their god to heed their pleas. But we do not have that fear if we are Christians. Our God is able, willing and ready to secure our salvation. His ears are tuned to our cries and if we heed His commands, we can be assured of eternal bliss in His presence. This eternal life is "in His Son" (I John 5:11) and if we are in Christ, we have this promise of immortality throughout the ages. Our baptism puts us in Christ (Galatians 3:27, Romans 6:3). And it is here that our salvation is secured.

We can see, then, the necessity of committing to God our past (He keeps it clear from the guilt of sin) : our present (He assures a fruitful life of peace and joy) ; our future (He insures good days upon earth for us) and our salvation (He secures the promise of eternal life in His Son). These are His share in the commitment we make. Now let us go to the human side.

WE SHOULD MAKE A COMMITMENT TO FORGIVE OURSELVES AND FORGET THE PAST. Too many Christians spend valuable time in worrying over their past life. They are too concerned with their mistakes and dwell on them constantly. Even when we have fulfilled the requirements for forgiveness and we know God has forgiven us, we still cling to a guilt feeling and cannot forgive ourselves. This is wasted time and effort. If God in His infinite compassion can forgive us, how can we allow guilt to rid our life of its usefulness in His service? Every moment spent in grieving over past mistakes means just that many moments lost to a present day opportunity. And we cannot afford to lose any time at all if we are to be profitable servants of our Master.

Paul accepted the futility of dwelling on the past when he wrote " . . . but one thing I do, forgetting the things which are behind, and stretching forward to the things which are before, I press on toward the goal unto the prize of the high calling of God in Christ Jesus" (Philippians 3:13, 14). Certainly we can profit from the past. But not by constant recrimination and guilt feelings. Only when we use our mistakes as guideposts to steer us from the same error in the present are we fully utilizing what has gone before. The past can serve to remind us of our constant need to trust in God lest we fall again but it is useless to try to relieve it or undo it. It is gone and if God has forgiven us, we have no need to carry the burden with us daily.

WE SHOULD COMMIT OURSELVES TO LIVE POSITIVELY. So many Christians lose the joy of the abundant life simply because they are so **fearfully careful.** Whenever an opportunity presents itself, they begin automatically to make a check list of why they cannot undertake it. And by the time they finish, the opportunity has usually passed on to someone else or gone completely. But they almost look upon that as "providence" since they had decided it wasn't feasible anyway. If ever the church needed the power of positive thinking and living, it is today! There is entirely too much of "We can't" and not enough of "With God's help, we can!"

Those individual Christians as well as congregations who are **doing** and **moving** ahead in the service of the Lord, are without exception the ones who have made this commitment of thinking positively and acting accordingly. They know **they** cannot possibly succeed in some great undertaking; yet at the same time they are assured that God can triumph. So they simply put their lives in His hands and through them, God works His will to accomplish whatever task lies before them.

Every facet of our life must be committed to Him. This means we cannot have a secular life and a spiritual life; but rather our existence is completely spiritual, bound up in Christ and secured by His promises. This works successfully whether we are a student who takes God to school with us; a housewife who seeks God in her daily housework and other activities outside the home; or a businessman who carries the Spirit of God with him into every walk of his career. The sooner we learn that we cannot live a successful Christian life by leaving God out of certain areas of our life, then the closer we will be to achieving that "life with wings."

The positive Christian life is that one which allows God to be at home in each distinct activity and area of our being. It is when we feel so at ease with God that our actions, our thoughts, and our conversations will naturally contain references to Him and His wonderful pattern for us. When we can talk unaffectedly about the "good news" to our contemporaries, we will have begun that positive life which carries with it the power to reach others with the Truth. Perhaps we do not attract others to our way of life simply because God has not made too much difference in our existence. We have not allowed His beauty to be seen in us and therefore, how can we recommend our way to others? When His beauty and the glorious joy of the life He promises can be seen by others, they will be attracted by what we possess. Then we can teach them because they can see the value of such a life of commitment!

WE SHOULD COMMIT OURSELVES TO A FAITH WHICH ALLOWS US TO LAUNCH INTO THE DEEP. Yes, I know the wise man counts the cost before he undertakes a project. I do not deny this premise. But how many of us spend our time in the "counting" department and never put the blueprint into production? Paul said he could do **all** things through Christ who strengthened him. II Timothy 3:17 tells us the Christian can be furnished unto **every** good work. Certainly we must be wise stewards in using what we have, but I fear the sin lies not in unwise use of our time and talents and money but rather failing to use them at all, because we are fearfully "counting the cost."

I am not recommending a rash, hastily conceived plan of work. But I do surely advocate a firm, sure step in the right direction. Many congregations and individual Christians think nothing of committing themselves to a huge sum of money for a building or other material possession. Yet if it were suggested that the same amount be pledged for God's use, they would be aghast! Material blessings are wonderful and can be used in carrying out the work of the church. But the mistake is made in placing too much emphasis on them instead of on the spiritual. After all, the material is temporary and will pass away; but the spiritual will go right with us into eternity!

WE SHOULD COMMIT OURSELVES TO WITNESS FOR CHRIST. Gabriel Marcel said, "I am obliged to bear witness because I hold, as it were, a particle of light, and to keep it to myself would be equivalent to extinguishing it." This should be our attitude toward the good news entrusted to Christians everywhere. We are told that we were won in order that others might be won also. Therefore when we become Christians we should automatically accept the commitment of witnessing to others.

Elton Trueblood in his book **Company of the Committed** puts it this way, "No one whose life has been truly touched by the life of Christ is free to leave the matter there; he must, as a consequence, extend the boon. If the enkindling fire (Luke 12:49) which Christ said He came to light has in any sense entered his soul, he cannot rest until he lights as many fires as possible. In short, a person cannot be a Christian and avoid being an evangelist!"

This is strong language but surely if we feel that the gospel is good news, how can we withhold it from a world which needs it so desperately? We are commanded to bear fruit or be cut off. And part of the fruit of the Christian life is the soul of another person won to Christ. We have become too apologetic with the Truth; we are constantly on the defensive. Let us free ourselves from the shackles of fear, pessimism and slothfulness and go on the offensive for the Lord.

Mr. Trueblood suggests a plan for the committed life which is four-fold—commitment, enlistment, witnessing and penetration. First, we must have the faith to place our life completely in the hands of God. Then we enlist in His service by becoming **involved** in the work of the church. This involvement carries with it the necessity of witnessing which is both personal and truthful. "I" know; this "I" have learned; here "I" stand. This is not hearsay testimony; it is first hand knowledge. A good moral life can be a character witness in this trial of life but it will never reveal the facts of the Truth. There must be that personal "I" witness. And wherever the Christian witnesses, he will penetrate that area of society with a leaven for good. And if enough penetration comes, the church will go to greater heights of service and the world could be changed for the better.

Faith, an unwavering, unshakeable faith, is the heart's blood of the committed life. Trust in God cannot be replaced with any kind of substitute. It must be implicit; it must be firm; and it must be the center and purpose of our life. Then we, like Paul, can say "I know whom I have believed and am persuaded that he is able to keep that which I have committed unto him against that day" (II Timothy 1:12).

TO THINK UPON

1. Are there areas of our life which can safely be omitted from the commitment we give to God?

2. What are some areas of fearfulness in this "total" commitment?

3. Discuss the providential care of God in our daily lives. Is it by miracle or natural process?

4. What are some of the dangers of hanging onto the past?

5. What are some ways we can be more positive in our life for Christ?

CHAPTER II

"LIVING WITH YOURSELF"

Wherever I have traveled in the past months; wherever I have spoken to groups of Christian women—whether in large congregations or small—I have found one thing to be true. **Christian women are eager and ready to be used in the work of the church.** And yet after talking with these women and learning more about them, I have found that many of them have not experienced the deep satisfaction of their Christian service which they felt would come. Most had thought that this gratification would come as a result of just being utilized in the work of the Lord. Yet it had not come to many and they are troubled.

The more we discussed this problem and analyzed the situation, the more we began to get just a glimpse of what could be at the bottom of their lack of fulfillment.

In the past ten years the church has just begun to recognize the value of what its female membership could produce. Congregations all over the country urged their women to be used in the many capacities crying for their service. A great untapped source of raw material was beginning to be utilized! And much to their credit, Christian women everywhere rose to the challenge!

She began to train herself to teach more proficiently. She learned how to do personal work. She gave of herself in benevolent work. Yes, Christian womanhood was coming into her greatest period of usefulness. BUT, surprisingly enough, she found that this service did not completely satisfy her. She became more and more busy doing more and more things —accomplishing much, it's true—but underlying all this, **she found that she hadn't yet learned to live with herself!**

And without the solid foundation this basic relationship can give to our life, our service to the Lord can never reach its fullest potential—both to others and to ourselves. If we are plagued with constant feelings of guilt; if we cannot respect our talents with humility, then we are in no position to really love and understand others. And without this love and understanding, our ministrations become empty as far as we are concerned. They might help others to a certain extent but they are profitless for us (I Corinthians 13).

Christ knew how important this relationship with self was. When He was asked what was the greatest commandment, He said "Love the Lord thy God with all thy heart, and with all thy soul, and with all thy mind, and with all thy strength" (Mark 12:29). And the next greatest commandment? "To love thy neighbor as thyself."

For years we have accepted this passage from the viewpoint that everyone automatically **loves** himself and should treat others accordingly. But more and more we find that this is not always true. For instance, if I have deep feelings of guilt over something and cannot forgive myself, this feeling will show itself in a critical attitude toward all I do. But it will not stop there. If I am very critical of myself, human nature being what it is, then I will feel free to be critical of others. It stands to reason that if I do not have the proper respect and love for self, then I cannot possibly have a true love and concern for others. Regard for another being does not rise out of nowhere. It flows like the pure water of a hidden spring deep from its source of inner "self-love." To assume that all of us love ourselves is looking at only one side of the coin. More problems than we know of can be traced right back to an inability to accept oneself and to live peacefully with that self.

Howard Whitman says that self-love is "simply having a little charity toward yourself, understanding that you, too, are just another struggling human, not making undue demands upon yourself—in short, giving yourself a break."

Dr. Robert H. Felix, former director of the National Institute for Mental Health, was asked how a person felt when he loves himself properly. Dr. Felix replied, "One has the feeling of dignity, a feeling of belonging, a feeling of worthwhileness, a feeling of adequacy—and a healthy sense of humility. He regards himself something like this: 'I don't think I'm the best person in the world, but I'm certainly not the worst either.' If asked, 'Would you want to be anybody else?' he would answer, 'No, I want to be myself.' "

So before we can start reaching out for the work which we can do as Christian women, I feel we should start at a more basic point. Let us take a look at the heart of the matter—me and you as individuals.

This is very hard to do because the world tends to try to lump everybody into some group or category. Republicans, Democrats; male, female; white collar worker, laborer; educated, uneducated. All around we are urged to conform, conform. Now we know there is good in some conformity. (The social courtesies and acceptable behavior patterns.) Yet in the final analysis of living here on earth, **I am me.** I must develop my own personality and act in accordance with my own beliefs. It takes courage to be an individual but it pays the best dividends.

Every individual has worth. God created each being as a separate entity—making no two identical in attitude, looks, or ability. There may be similarities but under close examination, every one stands unique. Each is responsible to God as a distinct being—and only for his very as an individual. My husband will not be judged with me nor I with *him* I will not be placed with the congregation where I worship and work (though it certainly might be safer for some of us if we could do this). But I will take **my** place before the Judge of all in that day and be rewarded or condemned as an individual. (And yet I cannot say we will stand alone if we are Christians. For then our Advocate, Jesus Christ, will be there to plead our case. But He will plead only **one** case at a time!)

With the evidence of such individuality, it is worthwhile that we take an inward examination. Pull the "stop" whistle on our busy life and retire to a period of self-evaluation. God's admonition to David's busyness was "Be still and know that I am God." Only with quiet introspect can we begin to be completely honest with ourselves and with God. Without the divine influence our inspection might only serve to drive us further from the proper self-love and keep us from ever attaining the full stature of gratification and confidence in our life of service in the church.

Therefore, let us as Christians ask the following ten questions of ourselves. The answers might serve to help in the appraisal of the "real" individual in each of us.

1. AM I HAPPY? Before we can give an honest answer to this, we must also ask "What is happiness?" Is it a person? A place? A thing? The answer must be "No" to each of these if we are to find ourselves on solid ground. For the first aspect of happiness which we must recognize and accept is that no **one**, no **place** or no **thing** can **MAKE** us happy! It must of necessity always come from within. If the capacity for joyousness is not within a person, there is no way he can obtain happiness. Too often we confuse happiness and pleasure. But pleasure can be purchased; happiness can never be bought. It must be **lived.**

True happiness is never something you can get directly. It is always a by-product of good adjustments and good living. In other words, live with yourself at peace and this will enable you to live at peace with others. One writer compared happiness to a butterfly. "The more you chase it and chase it directly—then it will always just elude you. But if you sit down quietly and turn your attention to other things then—it comes and softly sits on your shoulder!"

Man has been active in a search for happiness almost from the beginning but he always makes the mistake of trying to "find" happiness. He will try first one avenue, fail; then he will turn to another. Solomon, the wisest man who ever lived, was caught up in this same pursuit. He tried all of the ways which the human mind could invent to "bring" happiness—pleasure, knowledge, wealth, prestige—all failed. What was his conclusion then? "This is the end of the matter; all hath been heard:

*fear God + keep His Command
ments - for this is the whole duty
of man.*

It is interesting to note that in our translation the word **duty** has been inserted. But it seems to me that the passage would have a clearer meaning if it had been left out. To fear and obey God is the **completeness** of man. This is what will cause him to be happy and be at peace here on earth. This is why his Creator placed him here.

God's word gives us other admonitions toward obtaining happiness in our life. "Happy is the man whom God correcteth" (Job 5:17). "Happy is the man that findeth wisdom and the man that getteth understanding" (Proverbs 3:13). "Happy is the man that hath his quiver full of them (children)" (Psalms 127:5). I Peter 3:14 tells us we should be happy if we suffer for righteousness. These are only a few of the avenues which will take us in the right direction. The secret is to stop placing the emphasis on directly **getting** happiness. Just start down the road in the proper direction and soon you'll be in the right place.

2. AM I AMBITIOUS FOR LIFE? Do I have a zest for living? Am I enjoying my life? Certainly if we want to look at all the evil around us, we can say life is not good. But it is my opinion that too many Christians take this negative attitude. Yes, there is much evil and sorrow in this existence. But to say that life is horrible and bad because of this would be like saying, "One tree makes up the whole forest." Life is good and my attitude toward it can make me either ancient or ever youthful. It is possible to be old at thirty and equally as possible to be young at 80! It's all in whether we merely exist or if we really live.

As an individual, I am responsible for making my own world as bright and interesting and positive as I possibly can. I can either stagnate into a drudge doing the household chores or I can make myself a vitally **alive** personality. I can be interested in the world around me; I can be enriching my knowledge by reading, attending adult education classes or just by really observing all that comes in contact with me.

There is so much beauty in the world surrounding us. I often feel like the poetess Edna St. Vincent Millay when she wrote, "Oh, World, I cannot hold thee close enough!" Yet so often we fail to notice this glory of nature because something is hindering our view. How often do we stop to look at the truly exquisite "little" things which were put here for our enjoyment? Just this week I took my mother to the Chrysanthemum show at the Como Conservatory in St. Paul. We had seen these flowers before but I don't think I ever stopped to **look** at them. We slowly walked down the paths, stopping to really see the remarkable detail of God's beauty in these plants. Each petal uniquely formed and fitting in its proper place to make the whole pattern of loveliness! And how often I had missed this beauty simply because I didn't take the time to notice the little things.

Or perhaps I have been afraid to take the first step necessary to lead me to some new adventure of life. A recent article in **Readers Digest** called this attitude "Seeing Pitfalls Instead of Bridges." It told of a city girl who was visiting her aunt in the country. They were walking along a dusty road, hot and tired. The city girl was worrying about sunburn and the rocky road. The aunt suggested crossing a stream over to a small meadow but the girl gave all kinds of excuses why they shouldn't. The aunt took the first step however, and the girl followed. Over the hill was a meadow abounding in golden yellow daffodils! Did the young girl remember if she got sunburned or her feet got cut on the road? No, but she **did** remember that glorious field of yellow flowers!

How many of us are afraid of new, worthwhile experiences and begin to give all the reasons why we shouldn't try them? We fear failure; we fear what others might say about us; we fear being different. Whatever the anxiety, we let the opportunity pass us by and we are left behind staring at a pitfall, when we could just as well have passed over the bridge by taking that first step!

3. AM I SOCIALLY ADJUSTED? In other words, do I like people? It is a true saying that no man lives completely to himself. Every day our life touches the lives of countless people—a neighbor, a small child, a clerk, the milkman, the postman, our own family and friends. Yet do we look at each of these as a valuable source of good in our life? For we can truly learn something from each person we meet. It can be bad or it can be good but we all make our daily experiences a part of our being. To dislike people is to turn your back upon God. They are His creatures and we have no right to ignore the possibilities to learn from them or to serve them.

One common sign of mental illness is when a person wants to live a solitary existence—away from all life. There are many causes for this and we could not begin to adequately cover them. Our mental hospitals are full of people who have withdrawn from the world, not wanting any contact with fellow human beings. God intended we should live together, and peaceably if possible. Much of the Bible was written to give us an insight into how we can live in this world with other people. To desire a "hermit" way of life, wanting no involvement with anyone, cannot bring the abundant life which Christ spoke of. Learning how to get along with others; adjusting our lives to the problems involved; this is the beginning of brotherly love. Unless we love our fellow man, we cannot love God. Strong language but stated this implicitly in I John 4:20.

This does not mean that we must be social butterflies, flitting from one party or gathering to the next. No, there is a happy medium to be found. Enjoy others but learn also to enjoy **yourself** as a person also. We may know all the depths of another's feelings and personality but never even begin to fathom our own. Don't be afraid to be alone with yourself occasionally! Just as it is not wholesome to shut yourself off from the world, it is equally bad to keep yourself constantly surrounded with people. Learn to find time to be with your own company. Use this time to recharge your batteries—social and spiritual!

4. DO I HAVE UNITY AND BALANCE IN MY LIFE? A life which displays these characteristics is gained by a purposeful existence. A good personality and orderly thinking never come about by haphazard living. Goals are necessary if this life is ever to be achieved. An aimless drifting through life will bring us to a point near the end where we can see how little we have accomplished. Anything worthwhile is worth making plans for and keeping those plans in mind, work hard to attain them. The balanced life will show its unity in our purpose being put into action toward that goal we desire to reach.

First, there is no such division in life as secular and spiritual. If we divide our activities along these lines, we can almost be certain there will be an imbalance. Our life is either spiritual twenty-four hours a day or it is secular. There is no fence riding, half and half way. It is up to us to make the choice. Matthew 6:24 gives an excellent picture of the two possibilities we face and it also states that we can have only **one** of the two. If we are truly committed to Christ, then every activity of our life is carried out in a spiritual manner, keeping in mind God's way for us and our responsibility to Him.

Does this mean I'm to lead a sober, long-faced existence without any fun? Of course not! The balanced life is one that has a diversity of interests and some of these will naturally be on the lighter side. It means that our life will have a time to work, but also a time to play. We will be serious when the occasion demands and humorous when that is called for. Moderation is the keynote of this balanced life. Some work, some play, some study, some humor, some thinking. All these will fit into their proper place, not too much nor too little. Not overdoing one and ignoring another. Moderation, balance—this is the abundant life in action.

Being an individual is especially necessary in this unified life. I cannot possibly please everyone with my clothing, my abilities, my speech, my deeds. So I must learn to be myself, regarding other's feelings of course, but not trying to make myself over to be what others want me to be. If I have the courage to be a distinct personality, I must also have the courage to face the criticism which is almost certain to come. I should learn to profit from this—whether it be just or unjust. If I deserve the censuring then it should help keep me from making the same mistake again. However if I am not at fault, I can still learn from unwarranted criticism. I can let it help me look to the motives of those making it, trying to understand why they feel as they do. I can become more tolerant of them and perhaps make an effort to help them understand why I acted as I did. Either way, I can be a winner.

5. DO I GIVE ENOUGH ATTENTION TO THE PRESENT? The past is gone forever. I cannot change or alter it in any way. The future lies ahead. I do not have the power to project myself into it. Therefore it only stands to reason that all I have left to live in is the present. It is what I should be vitally concerned about and all my energies and purposes should be directed in making it the best possible.

We waste valuable time worrying over past actions, words and mistakes. We wish we had not done this or that; we would give anything to recall some words we said. But to no avail. Worry will not change what has already happened; neither will wishing. So we should be utilizing the time instead for seeing that those same things do not recur in the present. We are so often engrossed in the past that we make the same mistakes over and over again. Like Paul, let's learn to forget those things behind, and push forward to our goal! There are two passages of scripture which, if we truly believed and practiced them, w o u l d alleviate our concern about both the past and the future and would at the same time, insure our present of being happy and fruitful. Make Philippians 4:6 and Romans 8:28 a very active part of your life. If something can be done about a situation, be busy doing it. If nothing can help, take it to God and leave it there!

6. DO I UNDERSTAND WHY I ACT AS I DO? Are my words and deeds symptoms of underlying problems? Am I willing to be truthful about myself or do I cover up my attitudes and actions with excuses? "Ye shall know the truth and the truth shall make you free." We understand that fundamentally this means the truth of God's way for us and yet I feel we can apply it another way. **Only when we know and understand the truth of why we act as we do, only then will we be free of so many of our problems.** EXAMPLE: We constantly criticize someone who is doing a good work. Are we really seeing something wrong she does or are we jealous because she can do it or because they didn't let us do it? Too often we cover the truth about how we feel with a thin veneer of criticism or a superior attitude or perhaps even an inferiority complex.

We should learn to be honest about ourselves. If we do not like someone, let us not set about finding reasons which will help to keep us from disliking them. But rather let us look at the **real** reasons and start working on them positively. Tearing others down will only serve to keep us at the same level. For surely "those who sling mud will dirty their own hands."

7. DO I HAVE A CONFIDENTIAL RELATIONSHIP WITH SOME-ONE ELSE? Every person needs another in which they can confide. It can be a member of the family, a friend, or some other individual. But we all need to know that we have a place where we can discuss our problems, fears and our joys without being "double-crossed." It is a terrible thing to be lonely and know that there is no one to whom you can talk. Psychiatrists tell us that it is a universal need to be loved and listened to. And history, both divine and secular, is full of such human relationships. To feel secure in the concern of another is a great gift of life. To cultivate such friendship is priceless indeed!

But this confidential relationship is a two-way street. I myself must be able to accept confidences and to keep them safe. If I desire someone to listen to my problems and secrets, then I must be equally as available and patient in lending my ear to theirs. An ancient philosopher wrote of this association, "A sorrow shared is always halved; a joy shared is always doubled."

There may be no one to fill this void in our life, no matter how we try. Or else there may be certain times when a human confidante is not desirable or acceptable. These are the seasons when we can turn to our true Friend, the one who never reveals a confidence. There is nothing too large, no worry too insignificant, no joy too sublime that we cannot go to our Father, knowing that even when we do not have the words to express our real feelings, the Spirit is ever near to do it in our behalf. With perfect trust, we can cast our cares on Him, for He does love us.

8. DO I HAVE A SENSE OF HUMOR? Can I laugh at myself when the occasion calls for it? This is an asset which can serve us in good stead and help us through some otherwise trying situations. Can I see the humor in life around me? Surely there is so much seriousness in the world that we should enjoy the funny when it does happen. I'm not speaking of the cruel humor which so many present day comedians use at the expense of other people. Nor am I referring to the filthy humor which pollutes every media of entertainment — radio, television, literature, movies. But there is nothing wrong with enjoying the things in life which evoke a chuckle or two. Laughter is a beautiful sound and the ability to laugh is an asset in the abundant life.

9. AM I ENGAGED IN SATISFYING WORK? I might be an excellent teacher as far as theory goes, but if I do not enjoy teaching, this service will not bring real satisfaction to my life. With so many areas of work open to us today, we should not feel obligated to undertake a life's work which we dislike. We all need to feel this gratification in doing our job and to deny ourselves this pleasure will usually result in self-made martyrdom.

Of course we know that there are certain jobs we do because they are necessary. So we may have to learn to enjoy these chores which fall our lot. My mother gave her grandchildren Bibles and on the flyleaf she wrote, "The secret of happiness lies not in doing what one likes but in liking what one has to do." There is truth in this that can help us get through the many aggravating tasks which we must perform in our day to day existence. Our attitude will either cause the work to be drudgery or else a stepping stone to something better. We make the mistake of looking upon these jobs as our **duty** and this will do little to elevate our sense of accomplishment.

Today there is just too much to be done in the area of church work and in all this, there is bound to be something which each can enjoy and will bring them real job satisfaction. Because our talents are diverse, we can usually find that which we can do and which will also give us the compensation of feeling it is well done. Yet if unwanted tasks do fall to us, then we should be willing to tackle them with a more positive attitude. After all, life is not all doing what we want or like and the real success is the one who can not only work satisfyingly but who can be satisfied while at work.

10. DO I FACE THE PROBLEMS OF L I F E INTELLIGENTLY? Everyone has problems; this is not what is unusual about life. It is how you meet them that makes the difference. "Life itself is much like climbing a slippery glass hill. We climb, and we slip; we climb a little more, and slip again. WE ALL SLIP! Everyone has sorrow, disappointment, tragedy, frustration! But the real measure of the person is not **whether** we slip, but what we do when we slip. Do we pick ourselves up and go a little higher on the hill or do we lie there and whine or even go backwards into illness and nervous breakdown?"

DON'T RUN AWAY FROM PROBLEMS. We should learn to recognize them, evaluate them and then get to work on them. Many of our difficulties cannot be left behind; they go with us throughout life. But even with those we have help from God in meeting them. II Corinthians 10:3 tells us that God does not allow us to be tempted above that which we can bear and that with every temptation He gives a way of escape, **that we might be able to bear them.** For years I thought that this meant we would be freed completely from those temptations and difficulties. When I did not escape some of mine, I felt concerned and frustrated. A more careful study indicated that perhaps some do not go away from you. And the method of "escape" from those would be the ability to bear them. When I recognized this and began to find the ways to bear them, I was gratified to find this promise was true!

DON'T RUN INTO PROBLEMS. By exercising good judgment and perception, we can avoid many of our troubles. We have enough control over our life so that we can steer clear of a lot of these difficulties. When we are faced with a decision, there are steps we can take to help us make the right one. We can see what alternatives we have and the possible consequences of each. Then by prayer and good human understanding we can choose which alternative would be best and then set our purposes, goals and energies accordingly. This simple formula can do much to help us make the right decision which can keep us from a lot of problems.

Finally in this self-evaluation, we must realize that there will be some things which cannot be changed no matter what our course of action might be. These are the things we must not dwell on. If all our work, worry and action will not alter a fact, then we must learn to accept it, and live peaceably with it. For not until I have conquered the art of living with myself, can I successfully live with the world. I must accept my failings; accept my talents. Accept the good; accept the bad. I will change what I can but will live with what I am, knowing that peace within can never be forced from without.

Shakespeare summed it up beautifully in this passage "This above all: to thine own self be true, and it must follow, as the night the day, thou canst not then be false to any man."

TO THINK UPON

1. What areas of our own lives are we most critical of?

2. Why do you feel you cannot love your neighbor properly if you do not have the proper self-love?

3. List some ways in which people in present day America are seeking happiness. Discuss why they fail.

4. Make a list of the things which must be included in a balanced life, showing that this life can be spiritual in all the activity it participates in.

5. Why do our problems get us down? Discuss some ways we can better deal with them.

CHAPTER III

"THE ABUNDANT LIFE"

In the most recent census taken by the National Church Council, it was estimated that the church of Christ in America has about 2,250,000 members. We are the tenth largest religious body in our country. When we think of over two million souls won to the Truth, we are almost overwhelmed. Still we find that the church's growth is not keeping step with the population growth. When you study the church of the first century and how very rapidly it grew then look at the advantages which we have today, we are made to wonder just why the church is not growing as fast as it should. And why it does not enjoy a much greater reputation than it does.

This question is being pondered all over the nation as interested Christians come together. More and more time is being given to finding the answers. And there are several answers to this problem. But from my own knowledge of myself and of the other Christians living in the area I come from, I cannot help but think that perhaps the basic difficulty lies in the life which most Christians live.

I began to examine this angle of the question quite seriously and discovered something which most members of the church have in common. I found that we are patiently, almost "stoically" enduring this life here on earth while the gift of eternal existence with God is held before us as a reward. **I do not intend for a minute to minimize the importance of the crown which has been promised those who patiently endure.** But surely there must be something more to this earthly life than the semi-misery which so many Christians seem to think is our lot when we accept God's way.

Jesus was interested in the welfare of the human being when He was here. This was shown by His healing of diseases; the miracles of sight, hearing and restoring sound bodies. Our Savior was even concerned with the hosts and guests at a wedding for it was on this occasion that He performed the first miracle of His ministry. He saw the good qualities of little children and urged adults to appreciate these values. "I came that they may have life, and may have it more abundantly" (John 10:10).

I believe with all my heart that Christ was vitally interested in the happiness and well-being of the life which we must have here on earth **before** the eternity of heaven. A study of the lessons He taught reveals that many of them serve to help us in living a better life HERE AND NOW—how to get along with ourselves and how to get along with others. Maybe we do not win others to our way of life simply because our way does not have any appeal for them. Perhaps we should ask ourselves "Has Christianity really made a difference in my life? Do I have the kind of life which would recommend itself to others?"

The more I pondered this question and studied God's word for an answer, the more firmly I came to recognize that we tend to exist too much in a future eternity, rather than accepting the Christian life here on earth as part of that eternal life promised us by God. In the fifth chapter of I John, we find that God gave us the Spirit as a witness concerning His Son. The tenth verse of that chapter says, "He that believeth on the Son of God hath the witness in him. And the witness is this, that God gave unto us eternal life and this life is in His Son. He that hath the Son hath the life: he that hath not the Son hath not the life. These things have I written unto you, that ye may know that ye have eternal life."

Notice that all these references tell us that if we are **in** Christ, we **have** eternal life. Present tense. The last verse of the fifth chapter states " . . . we are in him that is true, even in his Son Jesus Christ. This is the true God, and eternal life." Eternal life is **in** Christ and since our baptism puts us into Christ, then we have eternal life now.

So it would seem that where we have missed the point is in realizing that this Christian life in the here and now is a part of the eternal life which God promised. True, it is the preparation part; the imperfect part limited by time and space and subject to pain and trouble, but I believe that a study will reveal that we are now living in the initial stage of the whole pattern of eternal existence, and that God intends His children to be happy, well-adjusted human beings.

Does patient endurance enter into this pattern of earthly life? Certainly, because this life, being hindered by the imperfections of time and space, will naturally bring a variety of problems which even Christians must face. But here again a study of God's word shows us not WHY we have these problems. Rather it reveals HOW we can live victoriously through them!

Then why do we have such a hard time doing this? It is my opinion that we struggle so because we have ignored the greatest help which God has promised us in living the abundant life. I am speaking of His Spirit. Every Christian knows Acts 2:38 and that this passage states that the Spirit is given us at the time of our baptism. But as a whole, the church does not study or discuss this subject. Why? Because everyone readily admits they do not fully comprehend it and because there is fear that someone will accuse us of "spiritualism." I feel that we must awaken ourselves to the need of recognizing the power and support we are missing when we discount the working of the Spirit in our lives.

I want to state that I believe in the **miraculous** working of the Holy Spirit! Now, wait before you accuse me of digression. Let me explain what I mean when I use the word **miraculous**. I know the Spirit does not overpower me and say, "This you shall do now at this time no matter what you feel or desire." But when I yield my will to God's and say "Here am I; help me make your will my will," then I believe that through the indwelling of God's gift, His Spirit, I can do things which otherwise I could never accomplish. To that extent it is a miracle to me!

Paul recognized the value of this great power living and working within him to achieve his goal. "I have been crucified with Christ; and it is no longer I that live, but Christ liveth in me!" This apostle also said that if any man does not have the Spirit of Christ dwelling in him, then he is not a Christian. In II Corinthians 3:2-6 Paul informs those Christians that they were an epistle written, not with ink, but with the Spirit of the living God. And that through that Spirit they can have all sufficiency—not of themselves but of the power of Christ. This unlimited power is available to those in the body of Christ but how little we utilize it!

The Spirit was intended as a definite help in living the Christian life. "In like manner, the Spirit helpeth our infirmity" (Romans 8:26). This passage also tells us that the Spirit makes intercession for us when we are inadequate to express our feelings. Then it closes by stating that we can be "more than conquerors" through the Spirit and in Christ.

The Holy Spirit should be an active participant in our life. It must be to produce the fruits spoken of in Galatians 5. "For we through the Spirit by faith, wait for the hope of righteousness" (verse 5). Therefore a life guided by the Spirit will produce certain characteristics. These are the "fruits of the Spirit" and are love, joy, peace, longsuffering, kindness, goodness, faithfulness, meekness and self-control. If these qualities are shown in our living, then we know we have the Spirit within us.

THE SPIRIT HELPS US WORSHIP ACCEPTABLY. We are commanded to worship God in Spirit and in truth. Too many of us try to interpret the Spirit part of this to mean with enthusiasm, or esthetically enjoyable. And this is partly true. Our worship must be exhilarating and uplifting. But there is something else. Dr. Grimes puts it this way, "This is no substitute for power of action resulting from worshiping in Spirit. Our worship is too often harmless, so gentle, so proper, there is nothing to remind anyone of that young man who strode the country side and talked with the people of Galilee in burning words, the kind of man who leaves you restless forever afterwards until you have found His God and learn to call Him Father too. Too often our worship seems to act as a sedative to send us to sleep on flowery beds of ease rather than to stir us up and irritate us and tell us to gird our loins with the gospel and go out with the light of that gospel and convert the world." To worship in Spirit must surely carry with it the motivation to be busy the rest of the week in vigorously living the commands of God.

THE SPIRIT HELPS US UNIFY OUR LIVES. When the Spirit of God dwells within us, our Christian life becomes a seven-day-a-week experience. We sometimes like to think we can compartmentalize our life into secular and spiritual areas. The Spirit does not accept this kind of dwelling. It must be as an active full-time resident or else He will make His abode elsewhere. Our life is either spiritual or secular. It cannot be both.

THE SPIRIT HELPS SOLVE THE PROBLEMS OF INDIVIDUALS AND CONGREGATIONS. Romans 8:26 gives us the assurance that we can depend upon an intercessor to help us when we face seemingly unsolvable difficulties. We may not even have the words to express our needs and feelings, but this should not concern us. The Spirit is there. When every Christian is producing the fruits which come from the active participation of the Spirit in his life, then peace and unity will reign in any group.

Let me say that I do not fully understand how the Spirit works but I do know that it DOES. Let us pray for a re-awakening of the vital necessity of utilizing this power in our lives. The supply is unlimited and always available. Our prayer should be as David's in Psalm 51:10. "Create in me a clean heart, O God. Renew a right spirit within me." Let us say each day, "Everything I do will be guided by the Spirit of God. Let my every action be governed according to His will." Then the abundant life will be no longer wishful thinking but a vivid reality!

What are some of the characteristics of the abundant life? What are some things I can do to help produce these fruits of the Spirit in my life? The following will be a list of practical positive suggestions which, when guided by the Spirit, can help us live that "life with wings."

LEARN TO ACCEPT YOURSELF. We will not dwell too much on this facet of the abundant life since the previous chapter was devoted to this subject. Suffice it to say that we must learn to live with what we are and who we are, changing those things we have the power to change and relying on God to help us accept and live with those facts which cannot be altered.

LIVE A SIMPLE LIFE. All around us the world is moving at a complicated pace and becoming more so with the passage of time. The Christian life should be characterized by simplicity—moderation in every area of life. Busy-ness is the besetting problem of America today. The Christian who does not heed moderation will find himself involved in a multiplicity of activities which tend to pull him away from his primary interests in life. I am not saying that we cannot be involved in civic duties nor that we can't have varied interests. We just should make certain that we do not complicate our lives to the extent that we forget our very purpose of being here. Several years ago I was on the verge of collapse. I was pulled in so many directions that my physical being could not stand the strain. I remember what the doctor told me and have tried to heed it since. "Find one activity outside the home which interests you more than any other. Devote your extra time to that. You'll live longer and happier." Well, there was no problem as to the choice—I knew I wanted to continue my work in the church. So I gave up all the presidencies, chairmanships and heavy responsibilities of the other areas in which 1 was working. I still participated but only in a minor way. My full attention outside my home was devoted to the one activity I had chosen. And you know, I'm still as busy (my family might say busier) but I no longer have that pulled-apart feeling.

This is not intended as criticism for those who can take on all these activities without batting an eye. It is meant to help those who have gotten themselves into the corner of hysteria because of all the complexities they are trying to shoulder. Simplify your life. Be satisfied with doing an excellent job in one area rather than spreading yourself thinly over a great many.

SPEND LESS THAN YOU EARN. One of the greatest gifts any woman can give her husband is the ability to live within his income. Specialists are telling us that American women are killing their husbands at a record rate by demanding an ever higher standard of living and pushing their poor mates to supply it. Financial difficulties cause more problems in marriage than any other thing besides sex. No matter what the "Jones family" might possess! If your budget does not allow you the same thing, then learn to be content without it.

THINK CONSTRUCTIVELY. When a woman marries, she tends to let her mind stagnate into a messy storage area for recipes, household problems, and petty grievances. A lot of us would be shocked if we realized when was the last time we really **thought constructively** about something. Certainly we must have a place in our minds for all the necessary things which keep our home running smoothly but if we don't let these just sprawl all over, we find we have an amazing amount of space left over for something else. We should develop the ability to store our minds with useful thoughts. This might take effort but would more than repay any time we might spend on it. For instance, we just might have something else to talk with our husbands about instead of the usual household problems. And wonderful too, we will not feel lost in a conversation when we do get a chance to go out.

There is much trash sweeping around our world today and if we are not careful, a lot of it can drift into our mind. The Christian must stand porter at the door of his thoughts. For anything which is less than acceptable will leave a mark of some kind when it passes through our storage area. We should read good literature, watch the best television and movies and guard against the evil in the conversations we hear. Our memory will keep at least a part of all it comes in contact with and thus we can see the necessity of only letting the pure and good pass through. "Whatsoever things are true, whatsoever things are honorable, whatsoever things are just, whatsoever things are pure, whatsoever things are lovely, whatsoever things are of good report; if there be any virtue, if there be any praise, think on these things" (Philippians 4:8).

CULTIVATE A YIELDING DISPOSITION. The human being is born a basically selfish creature and sometimes we never outgrow this tendency. Too many of us always want things our way or we "won't play." It takes a great deal of effort and energy to resist this urge to demand that all things must go the way we desire. So many arguments, so much disunity is brought about because we do not want to yield an inch of our stand. If this is a matter of doctrine, well and good, but most of the time it is strictly opinion. Who am I to say that MY opinion is better than all? If we would truly make an effort to see the other person's point of view, then perhaps we could more often see that they too have ideas. Putting Philippians 2:4 into practice would alleviate much of this selfishness.

LEARN TO "LISTEN" FOR LOVE. There was once a sad little girl. Her father asked her why she was so downcast and she replied, "No one loves me." But the father assured her this was not true and said that her mother had told her so at the dinner table. "I don't remember, Daddy, what did she say?" "She said, 'Don't eat so fast.'" The trouble with the little girl was that she was not listening for love.

Not many of us express our feelings with the positive words "I love you." Yet nevertheless there is more communication of love going on all around us than we are aware. But it comes out in different ways. To the husband it sounds like "I made this cake just for you." To the teenager, "Don't drive too fast and be home early." To the wife, "My, but this dinner is good." All these say "I love you" in the best possible way. We miss so much love simply because our radar is not tuned to the right wave length. Learning to listen for love will bring untold reward into our lives; so let's get that radar working!

BE GRATEFUL. The Christian life should be characterized by such a deep gratitude that we could not let a day pass without expressing these feelings to our God. Every day brings with it blessings which we could not begin to enumerate and yet we have the audacity to complain and grouch about so much. First, we have our homes. Are we grateful enough for them and the wonderful relationship contained within their walls? Then, our families. Do we thank God for them? What about just the "simple" thing of being alive? Surely we should feel like David when he said, "I am fearfully and wonderfully made." This piece of divinely engineered machinery we call our body is so marvelous that we should never stop thanking God for all the things it can do and enjoy. There are so many other areas—health, ability to work, our nation, the beauties of nature—how ungrateful we must seem to the Creator when we take these so much for granted.

RULE YOUR MOODS; DON'T LET THEM RULE YOU. We were created with an emotional part of our being. This can be either an asset or detriment in our abundant life. For no person lives on a completely even emotional keel. We have our ups and downs. Fear, joy, pain, sorrow—all come to us. The things which should set the Christian apart from those outside the church is the ability which we have, through Christ, to control our emotions instead of letting them have sway over us. But this takes active effort to keep those tricky feelings from coming up and taking over. Some of them we can allow more freedom; but others must be kept severely in bounds. It is up to each individual to control his own moods. If I am "down in the dumps" then I have even a greater responsibility to see that this does not spill out of control and "slop" over on others. I have no right to make others the victims of my moods. I may have to seek a place where I can recharge my emotional batteries when these times come upon me. But I must try to keep a balanced life by showing self-control.

GIVE OF YOURSELF GENEROUSLY. David Dunn has written a book called **Try Giving Yourself Away.** It's a valuable, inspiring little book and one which I highly recommend to all Christian reading lists. Mr. Dunn made a practice of finding ways to give of himself, knowing that nothing could be given, nor was expected, in return. This has made a marked difference in his life and he urges others to try it. Shortly after I read the book, I was in a trading stamp redemption center. I was waiting for my article when I heard the woman standing next to me talking to the clerk. "I didn't bring my purse so I don't have the 20 cents for the tax. I'll have to come back later." My mind began to whirr, "Give yourself away." I turned to the woman and offered the 20 cents. In shocked amazement she refused but I simply put it on the counter saying, "It will give me pleasure to do this for you." I took my package and walked out. I can still see the look on that woman's face and I like to think her day was made just a little brighter. I know mine was!

Seek ways to serve others; it doesn't have to be a big project. Perhaps you could take time to write a note to your child's Bible school teacher thanking her for the time and effort she expends in helping your little one. Express your gratitude for some good work of literature you've read or some excellent radio or television program you've enjoyed. Help an older person across the street or up the stairs. Hold a door open for a mother with a baby in her arms. Simple acts of giving yourself! Purchased gifts are nice and I'm sure they are appreciated. But the best gift of all is yourself, your attention, your concern for even a short time.

WORK WITH RIGHT MOTIVES. The thirteenth chapter of I Corinthians sets forth the ruling motive of the abundant life. No matter how much one can do or how many hours he spends in services to others, if his attitude of heart is not that of love, it will profit him nothing. This wonderful characteristic will be covered more fully in a later chapter so we will not delve too deeply into the need for love in our Christian service.

The "life with wings" should be motivated by the love God has for us which will then show itself in the love we have for our fellow man. Self-seeking has no place in this life. Praise can be accepted and can serve as encouragement to us, but it must not be the reason we are working in the service of the Lord. I can become great in the eyes of man, hiding the true motives behind my achievements. But God sees through this sham and is not deceived. If there is no love, I wind up a big zero-nothing!

BE INTERESTED IN OTHERS. If I possess this love, it will naturally follow that I will be concerned with those around me. In the degree that I give, serve and help will I experience the by-product of happiness. For true happiness lies in a selfless devotion to mankind. One writer has said that the greatest act of love is with-holding judgment of a fellow human being. All that I would like to say about this is summed up so beautifully in a poem by Mrs. R.E.B. Fielder of Van Alstine, Texas.

A Plea For Tolerance

Who could be so arrogant as to judge a fellow being? Before
One could judge truly he would have to know . . . .
All the diverse elements of heredity that through the ages have
blended to make of that one the personality he is;
The home into which he was born and if he were loved and cherished
So that he felt secure, or if

Matt 6-34 (one day at a time)

He were neglected, so that a sense of fear
And inferiority developed within him;
Who first told him of God, and if he believed,
And if he has ever learned to pray;
The books he has read, and the friends he has made;
The ease with which he fits into his world, and the efforts he makes
    to do so;
If his talents and abilities are in proportion to his ambitions;
The extent of his heartaches, and his capacity for joy;
Whom he has loved, and if he has been loved in return.
To judge truly one would have to know all of this and a great deal
    more,

AND WHO BUT GOD COULD KNOW!

LIVE ONE DAY AT A TIME. This, too, has been discussed in the previous chapter and yet it should be included in this abundant life. The past is lost; the future is only a promise; but today is real. Accept each day as a 24 hour gift from God to be savored and utilized to its fullest. Each of us is given the same gift and we can make it either worthless or valuable. If we could learn the lesson living one day at our best, then we would have our whole life made! We can do something for a short period of time that we would never tackle for a lifetime. Ask God to give us the strength to live this moment to His glory. He will, you know. And this moment will pass into an hour and the hour into a day. The day becomes a week, the week a year. A lifetime is made up of just years! So our life can be secured by living one moment at a time.

HAVE SOME TIME FOR YOURSELF ALONE. One of the most valuable books I have found is a small one by Anne Morrow Lindbergh. It deals with the conflicts in a woman's life and is entitled **Gift from the Sea.** In it Mrs. Lindbergh compares a woman to a water pitcher, sharing the good she contains with the world around her. But there comes a time when every pitcher needs refilling and this is when the woman needs to seek a time alone to let her contents be replenished.

As a Christian woman we are pulled in many directions — wife, mother, neighbor, worker in the church. And because we give freely of ourselves, we must needs make a time to quietly commune with God and refill our "pitcher." It may be only a few minutes but those minutes will do more to keep our attitude on a higher level and our actions positive. Do not be ashamed to seek this time away from husband and children. After all, you are an individual and as such, need to be aware of your own requirements.

DEVELOP AN INNER CALM. This is the peace promised in Philippians 4:6. For years I thought this peace meant freedom from problems.

And of course, I never found it. What a joy it was to realize that this meant, not the absence of difficulties, but the ability to face them calmly. In other words, no matter how chaotic the world around me may become, I can move through it without myself becoming chaotic. The abundant life is one of inner calm and serenity with the assurance that "all things work together for the good of those that love God" (Romans 8:28).

FINALLY, KEEP CLOSE TO GOD. This is a reality when you realize that He will come and dwell in you if you will only allow Him. Prayer is vital to the abundant life; without it there is no communication with our Father. Seek Him in the morning through prayer; give yourself to Him all the day. Nourish your spiritual self with His thoughts by studying His word. And know assuredly that He will protect, care for you and guide you into a richer life here on earth and in the end, to a blissful existence throughout eternity with all the saved before His throne.

The best evidence of Christianity is the Christian life. When we begin to really live the abundant life which Christ sought for us, then the church will begin to grow. For others cannot help but see that we have something which they do not. Christ has made a difference in our life and that difference is a well-ordered, full, happy existence. Christianity is not a set of rules but a complete way of life. When our life exhibits these qualities we can say to others, "Won't you accept the way of Christ as I have?" Then they can see the benefits which are the result of this obedience because our life is vivid testimony to the surety of God's promises.

TO THINK UPON

1. Have someone look up the scriptures which mention the Spirit dwelling in man. Discuss whether this means only through the word reposing in our heart.

2. Discuss the meaning of worshiping in spirit and truth. How does your congregation's worship compare to your findings?

3. Have someone look up what the early Restoration preachers felt concerning the Spirit. What was the attitude of other religious groups of that period concerning the working of the Spirit?

4. What are some ways the wife can help in the financial area of the home? What are the ways she most commonly hinders in this area?

5. Discuss "A Plea for Tolerance" in light of the racial questions of our day.

CHAPTER IV

"QUALITY CONTROL"

On a visit to Illinois I was given the privilege of touring a large pharmaceutical laboratory. We were taken through the plant, watching each operation in the production of medications. Every step was carefully executed in the most sterile and meticulous surroundings. We saw the raw materials start their journey to become a pill, a liquid medicine or a capsule. As we passed along I noticed that in every department there were workers who were taking some of the product off the assembly line. I asked if these were rejects but our guide said, "No, they are pulling those out to be taken to Quality Control." Of course I didn't know what Quality Control was so I asked for an explanation. The young woman was most patient and told me the following:

"Quality Control is a testing process whereby every product is tried and examined rigidly to see if it comes up to specifications. You see, our company's name is placed on every item produced here. That name has a good reputation and the buyers of our merchandise can be assured they are receiving a first class product. Therefore it is absolutely necessary that we take these samples from every step of the process. They are carefully tested to see if it is good enough to put our company's name on. By controlling the quality all along the line, our customers need have no doubts at all that what they are using is the best available. A medication must live up to our name before we put it on the market."

As we continued the tour and I saw more examples of Quality Control, I began to turn this practice over in my mind. As Christians we are passing along the assembly line of life. Should we not be as careful as a drug manufacturer that our "product" be of the highest quality? If we would be this diligent in examining the different "steps" or areas of our life, then we could be certain that we are worthy of the name we bear. **Christian** would be a respected and admired name because the "product" behind it would be living up to its reputation.

The more I thought upon this subject of Quality Control, the more I felt there was a basis for a similar procedure in God's word. Sure enough, I found that God is also interested in Quality Control. "Try your own selves, whether ye are in the faith; prove your own selves . . . " (II Corinthians 13:5). "But let each man prove his own work, and then shall he have his glorying in regard of himself alone, and not of his neighbor" (Galatians 6:4).

The Christian is admonished to "prove" himself before he eats of the Lord's Supper (I Corinthians 11:28). He is told that by rejecting the way of the world, he can be transformed by the renewing of his mind and in this way "prove what is the good and acceptable and perfect will of God" (Romans 12:2). But there are outside forces which God allows to help in the Quality Control testing of the Christian. Temptations and tribulations. Yet he is assured that this testing of his faith will serve to make him patient (James 1:3).

So with this command that we should try our way of life, I thought we might look at some areas which could be tested in a Quality Control test.

LET US QUALITY CHECK OUR OBEDIENCE. This should be the very first test along the assembly line because if our obedience is unacceptable, there is little use in letting the "product" go further down the system. The first trial should prove just whom I am obeying. "Know ye not, that to whom ye present yourselves as servants unto obedience, his servants ye are whom ye obey; whether of sin unto death, or of obedience unto righteousness" (Romans 6:16). It is impossible to obey two masters; I either serve God or I serve sin. My obedience is due the one whom I wish to be my master. Therefore, as the apostles, "I must obey God rather than man" (Acts 5:29).

My obedience to God will put my life on the right track and I can start the journey of the Christian life with the hope that He will grant me salvation because of my submissiveness to Him (Hebrews 5:9). I dare not follow another for what terrible things await those who obey not God (I Peter 4:17)!

LET US QUALITY CHECK OUR SERVICE. The Christian life is a serving way; we serve God by helping our fellow man. This means that I cannot separate my work into secular and spiritual; it must all be as service to our Father. Colossians 3:24 tells us that any work we do as Christians is unto God, not man and therefore the reward is from Him also. In other words, my ministration is for the glory of God. My whole life is imbued with His Spirit, therefore any way I employ myself is spiritual service.

This is readily seen in Romans 12:1 where we are urged to "present ourselves as living sacrifices for this is our reasonable (or spiritual) service." God does not want half-hearted, part-of-the-way servitude; He demands our very life as a vibrant, active sacrifice to His way. His Son taught this lesson when He told His followers they could not serve two masters. When we let our service be guided with love (Galatians 5:13), then it will be well-pleasing to God.

In quality checking my service I should not be so harsh as to expect it to be that which I cannot produce. God desires that I use my abilities but He does not demand of me that which I do not possess to give. My attitude should always be that which was spoken about Mary Magdalene who anointed Jesus and wiped His feet with her hair. "She hath done what she could."

In I Chronicles 29:5 David tells his subjects about the temple which his son would build for God. He wants to start preparing the materials for this structure and he appeals to the people. His ringing plea comes down to us just as sharp and clear today as when he issued it. "Who then offereth willingly to consecrate his service unto Jehovah?" And we can answer with even more alacrity because our service is in the "newness of the spirit, not the oldness of the letter" (Romans 7:6).

LET US QUALITY CHECK OUR ATTITUDES. My attitude can do a great deal to help me lead the abundant life. And yet a most common failing in the church today is the gloomy, pessimistic outlook of so many of its members. Christians should be the most joyously happy people in the world. Paul tells us in Philippians 4:4 "Rejoice in the Lord always; again I will say, Rejoice." And Peter wrote that we should rejoice with joy "unspeakable and full of glory" (I Peter 1:8).

There is much to be happy about in the life promised us. True, those in the world may fail to see the reason behind our rejoicing, but that is not important. They can tell that no matter what happens to us, we reflect a cheerfulness beyond their understanding. No one saw the Eunuch of Acts 8 go on his way rejoicing and if they had, would probably not have fathomed the meaning of his joy. Yet we as Christians can feel this same emotion because we **know** the freedom he felt, the complete release from the sins of his life.

The whole book of Acts pictures another reason for the happiness of Christians. They could even rejoice that they could suffer for Christ! Their persecutors surely did not understand their attitude—joy under such duress! Yet every Christian can possess this same glorious contentment which comes with knowing that "all things work together for the good."

I should quality check my attitude also to see if it is forgiving. A stiff-necked Christian is out of character and will be rejected from ever becoming a "finished product." I must be certain that I can show a forgiving spirit to all I meet—Christian and non-Christian. The absolute necessity for this is seen when I realize that my own forgiveness is based on my attitude toward others. It is sad, but true, that as we grow older we find it harder to pardon what people do to us, or what we imagine they do. It is also true that with age we become more easily hurt. This is a dangerous combination and one which Christians must ever be on guard against. How many of us will stand unforgiven because of a rigid vengeful spirit?

Another check point in my attitude should be on the optimistic scale. A great many Christians do little because they think little. They say "I can't" until they really believe it is impossible to accomplish anything. Even if they feel or know how they cannot achieve something, they have forgotten that **God** can and will work within them to perform great things. This fatalistic "I can't" should be changed to the positive, living "I can, with God's help!" Then really believe Philippians 4:13 when it says **all** things!

LET US QUALITY CHECK OUR THOUGHTS. We pay little attention to our thoughts because they are not openly visible to the world. Perhaps we think they are our own little possession, hidden from all others and therefore we need not bother to keep them "up to specifications." How mistaken this is! The wisest man who ever lived recorded that "As a man thinketh, so is he" (Proverbs 23:7). And the New Testament tells us that they are not so private as we might think for God is a discerner of our thoughts (Hebrews 4:12). So we should be most careful to pull a sample off the line and check its quality.

It is our deepest thoughts which turn us first to God and in controlling them, we are led to obedience of Christ (II Corinthians 10:5). After David had committed his heinous sin with Bathsheba, it was his meditation which caused him to seek God in repentance. "I thought on my ways and turned my feet unto thy testimonies" (Psalm 119:59). So we see it is necessary to keep a rein on this elusive part of our being. Without control, they can run riot and get us into all sorts of difficulty. The prophet Jeremiah said that evil came upon the people as the "fruit of their thoughts" (Jeremiah 6:19). What bitter fruit many of us will bear if we do not purify and protect our thoughts.

Our mind is a kind of memory storehouse of all that we learn. Everything that becomes a part of it does so through one of the five senses given us by God—sight, hearing, smell, touch, taste. Each experience involving these sends a coin to that storehouse and we are storing up a treasure. Yet the Bible says that this treasure can be either evil or good (Matthew 12:34, 35). It is the responsibility of each individual to see that the treasure of his mind is worthwhile and one that can be carried into eternity with him.

We have help in God's word on the positive things to keep our thoughts pure. We must not think too highly of ourselves (Romans 12:3). We must stand guard at our mind and let no evil enter (I Corinthians 13:5). And if these aren't enough, we are given a whole list of worthy thought projects in Philippians 4:8 "Whatsoever things are true, whatsoever things are honorable, whatsoever things are just, whatsoever things are pure, whatsoever things are lovely, whatsoever things are of good report; if there be any virtue, and if there be any praise, think on these things."

LET US QUALITY CHECK OUR SPEECH. We cannot utter too many words without letting the listener know what kind of person we are. Like Peter in Matthew 26:73, our speech betrays us. It is difficult to keep the real person from being revealed because our speech will only portray what we have stored in our hearts. Our hearts are the source of what kind of person we are. Therefore the quality check on our thoughts (heart) goes hand in hand with this test on our speech. It is difficult indeed to have one pure without having the other the same way. In fact, it would take more will power and control than most human beings possess.

We cannot take lightly the words we daily speak. They are being recorded in heavenly places and on the day of judgment, they will be played back—so to speak (except for those which have been erased through repentance). It is truly of great importance that we learn to control our speech. In fact, it is so serious as to be a matter of life and death. Matthew 12:37 states that we will be justified or condemned by the words of our mouth!

God's word has many admonitions to help us with our problem. (A later chapter in this book will be devoted to the tongue and its control). A lying tongue is one of the seven things which God hates (Proverbs 6:16-19). And in the same book, chapter 12:17 "He that speaketh truth showeth righteousness." The New Testament records that this truth should be spoken in love (Ephesians 4:15 and I Corinthians 13). This kind of speech is "sound" (Titus 2:3) and "seasoned with grace" (Colossians 4:6).

LET US QUALITY CHECK OUR COURAGE. Every Christian has probably studied the book of Acts more than any other New Testament writing. Yet how we can do this and pass over the examples of Christian courage in such a light manner, I will never understand. If we had to pick just one characteristic of the apostles which served them to good advantage in their work, I feel we would have to select their boldness. But, you say, they had God's help in making their stand. True. I do not deny this. Yet are we of so little faith that we think God will not help us show courage in making our testimony for Him? Fear does more to immobilize the Christian than perhaps anything else. Behind those fears must lie doubt, because if we truly loved God, these feelings would be gone (I John 4:18). When we feel less courageous, we should look inward and remove those doubts and renew our trust in God.

Paul wrote the Philippians that by his boldness Christ was magnified in his life. Paul had the courage to make a stand for the gospel and to testify of that position to the world. In this way Christ was better seen because Paul boldly brought Him forth to view by his preaching and his life. This bravery shown in our earthly existence will allow us to have boldness without fear on the day of judgment. (I John 4:17).

As Christians we are called upon to be witnesses to the Truth to all those around us. A timid witness will not be very effective; his testimony will be discounted by his listeners. Let us have the courage to step forth as proud attestors of the fact that Jesus is the Son of God and offers salvation to all those who obey. We have no reason to fear because Christ told us "I am with you always, even unto the end of the world." And one person and God is a majority any time!

LET US QUALITY CHECK OUR PRAYER. The Christian's prayer, like his worship, can become ritualistic if great care is not exerted to keep it in proper perspective. Christ taught a "model" prayer and sometimes we feel that we have found such a one for our own life and we use it no matter what the occasion. I Corinthians 11:15 commands us that we "pray with the spirit and with the understanding." This same order is given for our worship. So it would seem evident that God recognized that we could let our communication with Him become simply a religious ceremony, devoid of depth and meaning. When we look upon prayer as a direct line of conversation with our heavenly Father, then perhaps we can learn to utilize this privilege in a way which will enrich our life. Would you memorize a speech to use in a private conversation with another person? Of course not! Then we should make certain that our talk with God is carried on in a natural way, realizing that we are addressing a divine being as the only difference.

The prayer which Christ used in teaching His disciples contained the same elements which can make our own prayers acceptable today. Sometimes we make our request all one-sided—"Give me this" or "Grant me that." There must be praise in our prayers and thanksgiving, for our Father wants to hear these from us as well as the desires we voice. If we have been granted this blessed privilege of approaching His throne, then we should carry with us our feelings of exaltation and gratitude.

The Christian is commanded that his very life be lived in a prayerful manner (II Thessalonians 5:17). When we have sinned, we are instructed to confess these faults and "pray one for another" (James 5:16). In times of great joy, in times of sorrow or in times of illness, we have an avenue of release to seek the comfort and aid we so sorely need. Even when we do not have the capacity to word our expressions, He has provided that His Spirit interpret those feelings into an acceptable prayer (Romans 8:26). Perhaps harder than all to do, we are told to pray for our enemies (Luke 16:27). If God can love the weak creature we are, then surely we can extend that love to those who need our concern because of their sinful actions.

LET US QUALITY CHECK OUR GOALS. One of the most needful areas of quality testing is the goals we have set for our lives. Or perhaps the goals we have **not** set should be brought into better focus. So many of us drift through life, aimlessly moving along from day to day. There is a time of reckoning when we will realize that because of this carelessness, we have accomplished very little. For it is certainly true that unless we have a purpose in life, and actively work toward achieving that goal, we will finish the race empty handed.

It is also necessary to goals we might set to see if they measure up to the standard of the Truth. They must be worthy, but they must also be reasonable and attainable. But they must not miss the mark for Paul warned against the purposing according to the flesh (II Corinthians 1: 17). How can we make certain our aims are right? Solomon advised us to seek counsel to establish good purposes (Proverbs 15:22). We can gain much help from older Christians and above all from God and His word. "Commit thy works unto Jehovah and thy purposes shall be established" (Proverbs 16:3).

This committing carries with it an active participation in God's will. Like the prize in a race, the Christian sets his sights upon a high standard and faithfully runs in accordance with the rules provided. He doesn't look back nor to the side but keeps his eyes on the goal ahead. His attitude is that of Paul's in Philippians 3:14, "I press on toward the goal unto the prize of the high calling of God in Christ Jesus."

LET US CHECK OUR TALENTS. The parable of the talents in Matthew 25 clearly teaches that every person is given at least one ability. No one is left out. As a good steward, each must use that talent in the service of his Master. Sad to say, but too many Christians have failed to exercise their abilities and as a result, they are withered and dying. I believe the challenge before us today is to make our talents multiply for the Lord. For this parable also teaches that with the use of our gifts comes an increase many times over. We may have just one talent (I really doubt there are very many one talent only people!) but we should be busy finding ways to put it to use. We can be assured it will develop into another and still another if we just make that initial step of usefulness.

LET US QUALITY CHECK OUR INFLUENCE. One of the attributes given mankind is his influence. When it comes to him, it is completely neutral, ready to be molded into any fashion he so desires. But it doesn't stay harmless very long. We "rub off" on everyone we meet and this leaves our influence behind. We should realize that we have some kind of reputation with every one with whom we come in contact. It may be positive or it may be negative, but we are influencing some way constantly. Then our duty is to quality check that ability to affect others and make certain it is in keeping with God's standard. I can either be a great inspiration or a miserable stumbling block to my fellow man. It is up to me to choose which impression I will leave.

LET US QUALITY CHECK OUR LOVE. Love is eternal. Unlike faith and hope, it will carry over into the life we have after death. It is the most vital of all the qualities of the Christian life, for without it everything is useless and vain (I Corinthians 13). How does my love measure up to the standard? First, my love for God. "Thou shalt love the Lord thy God with all thy heart, and with all thy soul, and with all thy mind" (Matthew 22:37). This kind of devotion to our Creator will increase our capacity to love others. The more adoration we feel toward God, the greater our tenderness toward our fellow man. How can we know that we have this love? I John 5:3 gives a simple test. If we keep His commandments, then we have the assurance that we love Him. This is the primary quality check we make on our feelings of love.

The very essence of the Christian relationship is found in the love we have one for the other. Historians wrote of the First Century believers "See what manner of love they have each for the other." This will spring from a fervent heart (I Peter 1:22) and will cause those involved to dwell together in unity and peace, whether it be in a family or in a congregation. When we love others as ourselves (Romans 13:9, Galatians 5:14, James 2:8) our every action will be geared to the good of those around us. It cannot help but make our world better!

But Christ not only wanted us to love those who were lovable, He desired that our good will extend to those who were not so admirable. He commanded that we should love our enemies (Luke 6:27,35). This may be hard for us to understand because the word **love** is used today in an all encompassing manner. Perhaps we can see this more clearly when we know that the original language used in the New Testament had several words, all defining different aspects of love. And the word He uses in this passage about our enemies is not the feeling of emotion as in other relationships. Rather it is an experience involving the **will** of man. In other words, our will must not desire evil for our enemy. It wishes him only good and our actions are governed accordingly. We cannot have the emotional feeling of "love" toward those who despitefully use us, but we can have the will of "love" in our thoughts and deeds concerning them.

An inspection of my love will also test my regard for self. This is vital in living the abundant life. For unless I have the proper relationship with myself, it only follows I will not have a good association with others.

—44—

I must respect my abilities and have the confidence which comes from the indwelling of the Spirit (II Corinthians 3:4-6). I will do all within my power to protect my health, realizing that my body is the temple of God. I will not think more highly of myself than I should; but I will have a respect for the sufficiency God bestows upon me when I seek His will.

LET US QUALITY CHECK OUR SALVATION. It is extremely important that we test our salvation because if we have missed the standard in this, we have missed everything. The standard reveals that God is the Author of eternal salvation (Hebrews 5:9) and He has declared that this gift is to be found in His Son (II Timothy 2:10). If I have my salvation secured in any other place, it is impure and cannot stand in the final testing. Since my salvation is bound up in my obedience (Hebrews 5:9), I must see that I obey the rules set for me to get in Christ and obtain salvation.

I must have faith (Hebrews 11:6). This faith will lead me to repent of my sins (II Corinthians 7:10). But still I am not in Christ. What must I do next? I must be willing to confess my belief that Jesus is the Son of God (Romans 10:10). Then all that is left to put me into Christ and obtain salvation is baptism. I must be buried with Christ in the waters of baptism. There I come into contact with the blood of Christ, receiving the forgiveness of my sins. I arise a new creature, in Christ (Galatians 3:27, Romans 6:3). Is this the end of my salvation? No, for now I must begin the faithful, abundant life. When I come to the end of my earthly existence, after allowing God to work within me to secure my deliverance (Philippians 2:12, 13), my salvation will be final and complete. I will be given the crown of life and pass to eternity with my God.

We have only touched upon a few areas which we can test for quality in the Christian life. But if we have a constant awareness of the need for controlling the high standard of this calling, we will be sure that our life measures up to the name we bear. And with all boldness we can say, "Examine me, O Jehovah, and prove me. Try my heart and mind" (Psalm 26:2). Then we shall hear "Well done, thou good and faithful servant."

TO THINK UPON

1. Why is it so important to keep the quality of our life high in reference to the name we bear?

2. How is it possible for our obedience to be unacceptable to God?

3. Discuss ways in which our service could be brought to higher standards.

4. What are the primary reasons you feel cause Christians to be so negative in their attitude toward the abundant life?

5. Discuss the connection between the fears we have and doubting of God.

CHAPTER V

"A LIMITED VIEW OF GOD"

(These views taken from J. B. Phillips' book **Your God Is Too Small**)

As you cross the Mississippi River bridge from St. Paul over to Minneapolis, a large billboard meets the eye. Its message is at once startling to the mind for it boldly asks, "What will YOU do with Christ?" Each time I travel this street my thoughts are brought to focus upon this question and I ponder it for hours after. Truly this is the most important challenge facing mankind today. For the answer each individual supplies will determine his eternal existence. And every person will give an answer to this query in some manner or other.

Some will gladly accept His teaching and the personal indwelling promised by Christ. Still others will reject His commands, choosing instead a man-made set of rules. Some will turn their head and heart away and ignore Him completely. Yet by this very act of disregard they have openly made their choice to take a path opposite that of righteousness. No one can successfully ignore this question because in the final analysis, there is no neutral ground. All will be divided into just two schools of decision— accepted or rejected! For ultimately every one will answer what they did with Christ.

One of the saddest things, however, is the fact that even those who accept God's commands and obey them in order to become a Christian, do not have a satisfactory relationship with the heavenly Father and His Son, their Savior. They want to obey His standards but they are sometimes puzzled as to what role this divinity should play in their life. As a result, they never get to the point where they truly "know whom they have believed."

We understand that it is impossible for our finite minds to grasp a complete knowledge of the infinite Ones. Yet we have been allowed enough wisdom and judgment to catch at least a glimpse of Who and What He is. Since we are human, though, we do not always see an accurate picture. Our view of God is often limited. First, and rightly so, because God chooses it this way. He does not desire that we see Him face to face in this earthly existence. He deems it necessary that we have a different relationship. This limitation we can and should accept with the faith that some day we shall see Him and know Him fully. However, the second reason our view is limited is because of preconceived human ideas which try to "categorize" God or pin Him down to an absolute concept. The purpose of this lesson is to investigate some of the limitations which we place on our relationship with God and to see if, by eliminating them, we can draw nearer to Him.

CHRISTIANS OFTEN THINK OF GOD AS THE RESIDENT POLICEMAN OF THEIR LIFE. Many people tend to accept God as a nagging, inner voice which is constantly regulating their life. In other words, their conscience is all that they know of God. This is an extremely dangerous conception to possess and we can readily see why. The conscience is not divine; it is human. And because it is, it can very easily be perverted, over-developed or under-developed. Any of these will bring difficulties if we believe our conscience is God. The human conscience is affected by our upbringing, by training and even by propaganda. We can be schooled that something is w r o n g f r o m early childhood and our conscience will thereafter hold us in check in that area. Or we can be taught that some evil is acceptable and our conscience will give its approval from then on. An excellent example of conscience perversion was the Nazi youth program. These young people were drilled and educated until they could perform the most heinous crimes of atrocity against human nature and still feel no pangs of conscience. We find this same practice in our own country in matters of race relations, class distinction, and even religious differences.

To accept the human conscience as God is too risky. Of course if it has been schooled in the standard of His word and trained to know His will, we can listen to its proddings. But to rely on it as divine guidance will never allow us an exalted view of God. For who can truly worship a nagging voice as the Ruler of the universe? A policeman who forbids pleasures and strictly controls your actions is not an adequate view of God, for though His will does guide us, His rule is one of love and not a whistle-blowing dictator figure.

CHRISTIANS OFTEN THINK OF GOD AS A "SPOIL-SPORT." The idea of Christianity as a negative religion is too prevalent not to be concerned about it. Statisticians tell us we are losing 75% of our young people to the world and one of the primary reasons for this is the fact that we have brought them up to feel that our way of life is a list of "Thou Shalt Nots." Certainly there are negatives in God's way for us. But we sometimes emphasize only these and forget about the more numerous positive areas which give us true freedom. If our idea of God is limited to His vetoing our pleasures and activities, we cannot begin to have the abundant life. We must understand that while His law does forbid certain things to us, it has even more liberties. He is interested in our needs for pleasure, just as He is concerned with our spiritual attitude. But we should accept the knowledge that because He made us, He surely knows what is best for us. The way He has ordained for man to follow is the **only** one which can bring true happiness and contentment.

We should not feel that God surrounds us with prohibitions. Christianity is a living, positive, vital way of life. Eugenia Price has written a book for young people describing this life as **Never a Dull Moment!** It is up to us whether we emphasize the negative or accentuate the positive. "If ever a book taught us to be something, to stand and do battle, to be far more full of joy and daring and life than we could ever be without God and His Son, that book is the New Testament."

CHRISTIANS OFTEN TRY TO P I C T U R E GOD AS MAN JUST MAGNIFIED. Because our finite beings cannot begin to understand the infinite, we tend to fall back on known qualities of man to characterize God. Some of these are acceptable since all the good we know does come from God. But to limit God by just "stretching" what we know of man can cause problems in our life. For example, we know that God is our Father. Yet if we have not had a satisfactory relationship with our earthly parent, we may find it difficult to see the proper attitude of kinship between God and man. We might not understand that when the Bible teaches that God is our Father, it is the affiliation of love which is being stressed—not just the disciplinarian agent which our physical father might represent. To compare Him solely with earthly relationships would be losing sight of the true wonder and greatness of the affinity which God has for His children.

Our mind must be allowed to reach out and dwell upon the magnificence and glory of divinity. There is no way which we can fully understand, of course, but we should make an effort to cut the ties of worldly "designations" and realize that God is more than just a good man, magnified many times over. He is infinite, complete and far beyond all the conceptions we might have of Him.

CHRISTIANS SOME TIME THINK OF GOD AS THE "GRAND OLD MAN OF THE PAST." What picture comes to your mind's eye when you think of God? Maybe you do not have a clear idea but so often we see a venerable old man with white hair and beard—awesome, great and frightening. Most of the artists of all ages have pictured Him in just this way. And perhaps this is because we know that He is all wise and we tend to associate wisdom with age. Yet is God old? To think upon Him as ancient according to time immediately brings up other thoughts, however subconscious. With age as we know it often comes infirmity and an "old fogey" attitude. Certainly God is none of these. He is from everlasting to everlasting but does that denote age? No. He is timeless and as effective today as in "times of old." He is as contemporary with us as the rocket ships we launch to the moon. His way is as up-to-date for us as it was for Abraham, Moses, Peter and Paul. When we confine God to the miracles of the ancient days, we take the vitality out of the picture we must present to the world today. They must be made to feel that He is our contemporary and His way is as modern as tomorrow's science.

CHRISTIANS OFTEN THINK OF GOD AS A PERFECTIONIST. This idea of God can bring more guilt and unrest than any of the others. Can we be 100% perfect? No. Then what does it mean for me to be "perfect, thoroughly furnished unto every good work?" How can God command me to be perfect when it is humanly impossible? To understand this we must realize that while God is truly perfection Himself, He is no **perfectionist!** He does not ask us to give that which we cannot. So it would seem that an individual's perfection lies in doing the best he can with God's help.

Christ says "Come, **learn** of me." Perhaps that is the secret. To **learn** implies growth. It also implies making and correcting mistakes. Growth in anything is a steady, upward progress. I can never be 100% perfect but I can be growing in that direction. If I haunt my conscience with the idea that God demands 100% perfection of me, I can never be free from guilt for I will never measure up to that demand. Discouragement and false guilt will plague me and I will not be "growing" to the maturity of a full-grown Christian. God expects nothing more than this continual growth pattern in my life.

CHRISTIANS OFTEN LOOK UPON GOD TO BLAME HIM FOR PROBLEMS. Sorrow and evil come to all men. Just b e c a u s e we are Christians does not mean we will not have these setbacks which come with living an earthly life. So often when they do touch us, we immediately ask, "Why did you do this to me, God?" The blame does not rest with God; He did not bring sin into the world. Just because He controls the universe does not mean He causes evil to affect you. He might **allow** it but there is a vast difference between the two. When Job was so burdened with woes, he felt this same questioning. But God did not give him an answer. Nor does He tell us **why** these things happen. He does give us the assurance that we can live through them victoriously. If we have a constant attitude of blame toward God, we will find it impossible to worship Him acceptably for how can we worship what is a disappointment to us? And that will be what He is if we feel He is "picking" on us. A strong faith may ponder and think upon the calamities of life, but it will never **demand** an answer of God as a test of belief.

CHRISTIANS OFTEN THINK THAT GOD BELONGS TO THEM ONLY. This view is quite extensive in the church today. Let me hasten to say that we know that God **has** promised certain blessings **exclusively** to His children. But to say that He is not concerned with others in the world is making Him our God only. While we as Christians uniquely enjoy His forgiveness and the salvation of our soul, God's love and care is not limited to us. He sent His Son to die on the cross because He did not want anyone to perish. Does this sound as if He had no concern for those outside the church? He causes it to rain on the just and the unjust. Does this not show He does send **some** blessings on the lost too?

A study of His word readily teaches that unless man obeys God's commands, he cannot expect to obtain eternal life in heaven. These commands include all the steps necessary to make us members of His body, thereby obtaining our salvation. But there are other elements of Truth in the Bible in addition to those which lead us to become Christians. Any part of the Truth that is taken into a person's life cannot help but make him better and point him toward happiness. IT WILL NOT SAVE HIS SOUL UNLESS HE OBEYS ALL THE TRUTH, but it can bring certain earthly rewards to his life. God's Truth is universal and will help all who heed it. It must be obeyed fully before eternal redemption is secured, but any part of it does bless the one who applies it to his life.

CHRISTIANS OFTEN THINK OF GOD ONLY SECOND - HAND. These are the people who, though they have obeyed the plan of salvation, never again personally seek to study His word to find His will for their life. They listen to what the preacher or the teacher or their family or a friend reveals to them of God. True, they may learn something about God this way, but they will never have the first-hand personal relationship so vital in living the Christian life. They do not seek Him on their own, but rely on others' association with God to give them the needed help. They cannot see Him as real because they do not have a direct dependence upon Him. They remain uncommitted in a loosely connected link to a God they do not really know.

We might ask ourselves if we **can** know God. Since God is real, how can we know Him? He knew of our difficulties in this matter and because He loved us and wanted us to know more about Him, He sent His Son to earth. We can know more about the Father by coming to know the Son. We've never seen God; no man has. But many saw Jesus and because this divine being came to earth, it has never been the same since. He brought with Him a way of life which "turned the world upside down." Wherever His commands were obeyed, people found their lives being changed into powerful channels of good.

Many did not know God because they failed to recognize His Son. Their preconceived ideas of the Promised One did not match the qualities which God showed in His Son. They had set certain standards but Christ did not measure up to them. They wanted their ideas of the Messiah to be what God would send. But God does not need man's puny efforts. He revealed the divinity of Jesus by qualities which did not fit into man's conception. Mr. Phillips lists some of these in his book and I am including them here for our study.

1. He challenged the current moral values accepted by man.

2. He was concerned with motive as well as performance.

3. He insisted on real values—particularly on love. (Love toward God cannot exist without love toward man).

4. He taught that serving others is the best way to serve God.

5. He appreciated the beauty of nature, family life, childhood.

6. He did not go about "denouncing" sinners. His sincere concern for the sinners' condition was enough to show them the errors of their way.

7. He conflicted with man's idea of religion.

8. He called on all who could listen to re-center their lives on the real God, instead of on things for themselves.

9. He desired the companionship of the lowly and the lonely. They were the ones who needed and accepted Him for what He was.

10. He excluded the cares of the world from His life and yet He made the greatest contribution to man. "I came to serve."

Christ was not just a man **pretending to be God.** He was God come to earth. The Father manifested His love for His earthly creatures by sending the Son to live in the same walk of life. He let man know Who He was and What He was by revealing Himself through Christ. We can never come to God without first knowing and coming through Jesus.

And this coming through Christ involves the total commitment of our life. To many Christians the way Christ brought has become a mere set of rules. But Mr. Phillips states "to those in the first century it was an invasion of their lives by a new quality of life altogether. They were so convinced of their God and His way, that they no longer felt they belonged to themselves. They were committed to tell of this way to others. They **knew** God because they knew His Son and what He had brought to them—the salvation of their souls and a way of life so dynamic that they could not keep it to themselves. Their limited earthly existence took on a new meaning because now they were linked with an unbreakable tie to the greatness and glory of God. They did not know Him face to face in their mortal life, but some day in immortality they would!"

DO YOU KNOW GOD? WHAT ABOUT YOUR HOPE TO SOME-DAY KNOW HIM FACE TO FACE? Let us cast off the negative limitations we have placed on God and allow our hearts to soar up to the height of His greatness, the wonder of His goodness, knowing that while we can never see Him fully, we can come closer because of the promises granted by His love for us.

TO THINK UPON

1. Why is it dangerous to "let our conscience be our guide?"

2. What are some of the ways we can be more "positive" in our teaching of the Christian life to our young people?

3. Discuss the differences between age according to time and age according to eternity.

4. Since so many religious groups feel the church should be "updated" how can we prove its message is contemporary for us as it is?

5. Discuss the difference between the ideas man had about the Messiah and the qualities Jesus actually showed.

CHAPTER VI

"THE HARDEST JOB"

One of the first things which a physician says to his patient is, "Let me see your tongue." A spiritual advisor might well do the same because much "illness" in the Christian life can be traced right back to the speech uttered by this small member of the physical body. A physician does not look at the tongue because of any disease which that organ might have; he knows that it is a good indicator of sickness in other areas of the body. And the same is true of the spiritual realm. While we recognize the fact that certain speech is sinful, we should also realize that it is usually a manifestation of a greater evil which is affecting the heart.

Speech is one of the greatest gifts of God to mankind. Daniel Webster said, "If all my talents and powers were to be taken from me, and I had my choice of keeping but one, I would unhesitatingly ask to be allowed to keep the power of speaking, for through it I would quickly recover all the rest." How wonderful it is to be able to communicate with our fellow man by the marvelous ability of speech! Yet, of all the blessings granted us by our Creator, this one is probably misused more than all the others put together. A group of preachers were asked to name the sin which they felt would cause more Christians to be counted lost in the day of judgment. Without exception they answered "The sins of the tongue." Of course we understand these ministers will not be judging us in that day, but their unanimous opinion should be a warning.

Just how serious is this matter of the tongue we see in Matthew 12:36, 37. "And I say unto you that every idle word that men shall speak, they shall give account thereof in the day of judgment. For by thy words thou shalt be justified, and by thy words thou shalt be condemned." Frightening, yet these were the words spoken by Jesus and we must believe that He means what He said. James 3:8 calls our tongue a "restless evil, full of deadly poison." This is an apt description because nearly all of us can testify to the difficulty of controlling the words of our mouth. How easy it is to let them pour forth and yet we should realize these venomous words are compared to deadly poison. And worse than destroying the physical body, they have the power to destroy the effectiveness of our religion. "If any man thinketh himself to be religious, while he bridleth not his tongue but deceiveth his heart, this man's religion is vain" (James 1:26).

James also tells us that the tongue cannot be tamed! And if this was his only statement we could have no hope. But he gives us reassurance, too, for he says it **can** be bridled or controlled! We might bring a wild beast into our home and keep it as a pet. By our love and care we may be able to control its native instinct for viciousness. But if we relinquish that constant attention over it, almost without exception such an animal will revert to its wild nature. We should think of our tongue in just such a manner. By constant care, tempered with love, we can keep our speech harmless and enjoyable. But ignore that carefulness and it, too, will revert to its wild nature!

In this study of the tongue, we will take the negative side first. Not because of any desire to condemn ourself and others, but in order that we can close the lesson with the positive picture of this gift. It is always pleasant to leave a meal or a conversation with a sweet taste. Just so this lesson. I know we will find ourselves among the bad points because we are human. Yet I feel that we should not close a lesson with that view, for I'm certain we will recognize some of the good we have also. And commendation serves as an incentive to try even harder to eliminate the negative and emphasize the positive!

THE TONGUE IS COMPARED TO A HORSE BRIDLE IN JAMES 3:3. When I was quite young and we lived in the country, horseback riding was about my favorite pastime. I would often go up to the field and calling the horse to me, climb onto his back. Clutching his mane, I would try to guide him toward the barn. I was not often successful unless the horse really wanted to go that way. But if I took the bridle with me and slipped the bit in his mouth, I could jump on and he would take me where I wanted to go. I recall one time while galloping down the road, the halter broke at the bit ring. The bit slipped from the horse's mouth while we were traveling full tilt. Feeling his freedom, my mount started a chase which ended with me falling off amid the rocks and weeds. I shall never forget the sickening feeling of fright in that uncontrolled ride and believe me, I was grateful to come away with only scratches and bruises! Yet how many times have I let the "bridle" slip from my own mouth and away rushed my words, uncontrolled and wild!

And what is the bridle which helps us control our tongue? I would say it had three main parts. First, love. Second, prayer. And third, self-control through the help granted us by Christ.

THE TONGUE IS COMPARED TO A SHIP'S RUDDER IN JAMES 3:4. I am not much of a sailor. It isn't that I'm exactly afraid of the water but rather that I possess a healthy respect for it. And when I am out in a boat, you can be assured I want that water vehicle to get to its destination safely, without aimless and dangerous wandering all over the lake. Those who know about these things tell me that the rudder is a most important part of a ship. Even in the most stormy seas, that little piece of equipment serves to keep the whole ship in the right direction, bringing it to port safely. So, though the tongue is little, it can do big things also. It can be controlled to take us through the stormy times serenely or it can be given its way and we will be driven before the winds of evil and danger on the sea of life.

What are the best materials to be used in this rudder? Surprisingly enough, a bridle and a rudder can very well be made from the same things. Love and prayer and self-control with the help of God.

THE TONGUE IS COMPARED TO A FIRE IN JAMES 3:5. One night as the family drove to the mail drop, we saw a vivid orange glow in the sky. Following this sign we went along a country road and passed across the river and over the hill beyond. As we topped the rise, we saw an uncontrolled field fire sweeping across the land. It was an awesome sight and we could not help but think of the destruction it was causing. County firemen were later able to extinguish it but the marks left by its ravaging march are still visible.

James compares the tongue to this and because its fire is set by hell, it will defile our whole body and perhaps destroy innocent bystanders. To sustain our use of the evil of gossip we sometimes say, "Well, where there is smoke, there must be some fire." And this may be true, but usually the only fire is that of malice. William George Jordan says that malice is "the incendiary firing of the reputation of another by the lighted torch of envy, thrown into the innocent facts of a life of superiority." In other words, we are jealous because we cannot attain to the high qualities of another, so we begin to ruin that superior life by the sin of gossip and slander.

How can the fire caused by the tongue be contained? Again with those same versatile materials as before—love, prayer, and self-control with the help of God. Since we can see the danger of an uncontrolled tongue, let us examine some of the sins which are caused by allowing our words to have a free rein. Unless they are controlled, we can lose our eternal destiny with God.

SOME SINS OF THE TONGUE ARE DIRECTLY AGAINST GOD. Of course, every sin committed is a disobedience of God yet there are specific things which we can do against the very being of our Father. Blasphemy is one of these. This happens when one utters wicked, defamatory words against God. Only in very extreme cases does a Christian commit this openly. But there is a danger of unconscious blasphemy by failing to take seriously the sacred things of the Christian life. Some Christians do commit this kind of act without really being aware of what they have done—especially young Christians. For example, mocking the

Lord's table, the position of the elders, prayer, or making light of any Christian attitude which demands a serious mind.

SWEARING AND CURSING ARE A FORM OF BLASPHEMY. In the nation of Israel the Jewish people held the name of God in great respect. When they prayed, they would not even utter the sound of His name, feeling unworthy for it to touch their lips. Secular history tells us that instead of speaking God's name, the Jews would cross their arms on their breast and lift their eyes to heaven. Even in their writings the scribes would feel unworthy to write His name and would use a certain symbol. As a result, we are told by their historians, that God's name was almost lost to mankind because His people felt undeserving of even speaking or writing it. But how time has changed all that! Walk down any street today or listen to groups of people and you will hear that wonderful name being bantered about in a light and irreverent manner. Sad to say, even Christians are guilty of taking God's name in vain or swearing by it in an unholy manner. The Ten Commandments informed the Jewish people that those who use God's name lightly would not be held blameless. The same principle is applicable in the Christian age. We are given instructions in Christ's model prayer to hallow that name. To hallow means to sanctify and this would forbid the cursing and swearing we hear so much today. It is also the name in which we are to pray (John 14:13). Remission of our sins is granted in His name (Luke 24:47). The name of God and His Son are precious and valuable to those who believe. They should never be uttered in any way except honor, praise and glory.

Not many Christians commit sins of the tongue directly against God. But the same cannot be said about their words against a fellow man. For the largest number of speech transgressions are those involving another human being. Let us look at some of these.

EVIL SPEAKING. Ephesians 4:29 states "Let no corrupt speech proceed out of your mouth, but such as is good for edifying as the need may be, that it may give grace to them that hear." If we should heed this scripture, the rest of this lesson could be done away with. Evil speaking, or corrupt speech, must include all the complaining, bickering and unkind words which we utter day by day. Too often we feel that such "little" things are not evil. Yet the passage in Ephesians leads us to believe that our speech must be edifying and give "grace" to our listeners. How much do we speak that, while it might not be harmful, is certainly unnecessary? Nor does it serve to edify or build up the one who hears it. Babcock wrote, "When I want to speak let me think first. Is it true? Is it kind? Is it necessary? If not, let it be left unsaid." Those things which cannot pass these tests would well be left unuttered.

LYING. The world today would have us believe that there are different shades of the truth—a white lie, a gray lie, a black lie. But God's word does not give us any such comfort. I John 2:21 says that no lie is of the truth. So we can conclude that so much of what our society would shade off into respectability is nothing more than a deviation from the truth—lies, in plain language. We are commanded not to lie for the truth is the basic foundation of life in Christ. Yet many Christians do not heed the warnings against those who step over, or around, the truth. Gross exaggerations, which lead the listener to a mistaken idea, can be included in our list of lies. Those who use this technique state they are merely "stretching" the truth. We are victims of this in much of today's advertising. I am amazed at the ads we witness on television and read in the papers and magazines. Our nation has an agency to control false advertising but so often those who are brought before it are acquitted, saying they are not lying but just "stretching" the facts. We should remember that man's laws are not God's laws and even though man might permit such error, God will not.

It has been said that "lies are like peanuts. You can never stop at one." How true this maxim is! You cover up a mistake by telling a lie. But you will soon find yourself telling another to cover up for the first and so on until your life is an intricate network built on falsehoods. The sad part is that the revealing of just one lie will bring the whole structure tumbling down on you.

Some pride themselves on always telling the truth, no matter who might be hurt. Now, I am not advocating lying or misrepresenting the facts. I do state, however, that some rightful facts need not be uttered. For example, we are able to see that our friends new baby has unusually large ears. This is a true fact. Yet, to express this to the doting mother will not serve any worthwhile purpose. It may very well lose you a friend! So, just because something is the truth, does not automatically give us the right to publish it abroad. Your husband may have some terrible fault. Telling this truth to a neighbor may cause him a great deal of anguish. The friend could lose respect for your mate and in the end his Christian influence would suffer. Of course, you must not **lie** about these facts but there are times when the truth can be left unsaid.

SLANDER AND GOSSIP. It has been said that men talk about things but women talk about people. More homes have been broken; more lives have been ruined; more deaths have been caused; all because some person could not contain some facts they knew, or thought they knew. A lot of women defend themselves by saying, "Gossip is passing on untrue facts. What I'm saying is completely right." I don't know if the dictionary will bear out this definition but I am assured that God does not. To pass on some knowledge about another without a purpose of love behind the act is to seriously damage that person's influence and could be the cause of one losing his soul. The reputation is a very fragile thing. It can be shattered and the life ruined even if the person is completely innocent. To slander another is to affect his reputation and once broken, it can never be put together again without the scars of the break showing.

One of the Christian's most valuable assets in living the abundant life is his reputation. Our service in the church can be either hindered or glorified by the depth of our influence. When you damage my reputation, you could very well be closing doors of opportunity for me which can never be opened again. Even a small hint of slander can damage the respect a Christian has in the community. For human nature will more readily believe that which is evil and even when the true good is placed before them, the hint of evil still remains in their mind. There may be times when certain facts must be passed to another—to an elder or minister or loved one—in order to help safeguard the soul of a person. Yet even when this is necessary, it should be undertaken only after much prayerful consideration and love toward that other one.

Sometimes the person who listens to slander and gossip can be just as guilty as the one revealing the item. They usually have enough forewarning to say they don't really care to hear it. For the gossip is often prefaced by "I'm not one to gossip but . . ." or "Have you heard about . . ." How much damage we could end right there by refusing to listen! Even if we never pass the information to someone else it has deposited itself in our mind and could very well affect our relationship with the one involved. To be the bearer of tales or the listener can place us in jeopardy of losing our soul.

FAULT-FINDING AND UNJUST CRITICISM. Perhaps this is the most prevalent sin of the tongue in which Christians indulge. For we can find more excuses to justify our criticizing another. One of the most aggravating problems which elders face is this constant fault-finding of any program of work brought for consideration. Just criticism can be accepted and even serve to profit one, but there is seldom protection from the fiery darts of complaint and criticism merely for the sake of finding fault. It is inevitable that criticism will come if you are doing anything at all. This is a fact of life and the sooner you learn to live with it, the more serene your life can be.

THE FAULT-FINDER INJURES HIMSELF. You cannot sling mud without getting some on your own hands. How does this affect the slinger? The more fault we find in others, the less we find in ourselves—supposedly. A good example of this is found in Matthew 7:3-5 where we are given the lesson of trying to take the mote from our brother's eye while we have a beam in our own. This is made more vivid when we understand the comparison of the two words, mote and beam. Mote is a small speck of sawdust while a beam is a huge plank. We are blinded to the fault in our own life when we try to bring attention to the problem in another's. The Pharisee in Luke 18:10-12 condemned his own soul because he felt he was better than the publican. Psychologists tell us that the fault-finder is trying in some vicarious way to build his own stock to a higher quality by tearing down the reputation of someone else.

THE FAULT-FINDER HURTS THE ONE HE CRITICIZES. Psalms 64 pictures the reckless talker as shooting arrows at his victim. The arrows used are sharp, bitter, poisonous words. They damage and injure just as surely as a steel-tipped barb will pierce the physical body. Fault finding hurts the person's feelings, his reputation, his usefulness and perhaps will even affect his eternal destiny. Can we afford to take the responsibility of doing any of these?

THE FAULT-FINDER SINS AGAINST SOCIETY. Constant criticism destroys confidence in the one criticized and confidence is a very important stone in the foundation of society. This is true in the church also. We can undermine the value of our leadership and affect our standing in the community if we are constantly censuring the church, its leaders and its members. Some congregations have no influence in their area because their memberships spread abroad great criticism of all they represent.

WAYS TO TAKE CRITICISM. Accept a certain amount. If you're busy, you'll be criticized. Examine it to see if it can be helpful. Do your best to make others understand why and what you're doing. Don't let your critics cause you to quit doing good. Don't fall into self-pity because others misunderstand and find fault.

THERE ARE MANY CAUSES F O R TONGUE TROUBLES. We could write several volumes on the causes of these sins and then probably never enumerate them all. However, we shall look at a few reasons and perhaps help in combating this disease of the spiritual body.

1. FRUSTRATION. We cannot control ourselves and we vent our feelings in words. Frustration carries with it the fact that we cannot accept ourselves for what we really are and beset by all the problems and difficulties of life, we take a step backward into confusion and despair instead of that forward motion toward peace and serenity. There should be no worry or frustration in the life of the Christian. Philippians 4:6!

2. SELFISHNESS. This is an inordinate love of self, causing us to desire the hurt and insufficiency of others. We are happy when others fail, or when we would like to make people think they fail. We build

ourselves up at the expense of others. This attitude nearly always shows itself in criticism and complaint, while making excuses for self.

3. INCONSISTENCY. We say we believe God but we do not have enough faith to take Him at His word. We practice what we want to and ignore that which we don't like. This brings about an attitude of trying to conceal when we don't measure up to the standards of the Bible. Lying most usually characterizes this trait.

4. FALSE PRIDE. We know we must have **some** pride in our abilities and a confidence in living the abundant life. Yet being human we too often build our ego way beyond the natural pride and into the puffed, false variety. This trait will also lead to fault finding and slander if we are not careful.

5. IMMATURITY. Little children say just about what comes to their mind. They have not matured to the point where their judgment controls their speaking. Many people beyond the childhood stage in years are still behaving in a juvenile manner of life. Immaturity in the Christian life will cause us to commit sins of the tongue, perhaps even without realizing they are transgressions. Here again we see the necessity to study God's word in order that we might mature into a full-grown Christian, able to control our actions and speech.

6. JEALOUSY. Envy and jealousy will most often find their outlet in vicious words against those superior to us. We do not like these attitudes and therefore we tend to rationalize our actions to be something else. Yet if we were completely honest, jealousy would be found at the heart of many of our problems of the tongue. It takes abundant love and prayer to help overcome envy and unless it is conquered, we cannot spend eternity with God in heaven.

We have only covered a few of the underlying diseases which erupt in sins of the tongue. They are enough, however, to let us see how vital it is that we constantly be on the alert to keep our speech under control. These are the negative aspects of this wonderful ability which God granted man. And troublesome as they are, we can still put them under subjection and emphasize the more beautiful qualities which should characterize our words.

SOME PROVERBS CONCERNING THE CONTROLLED TONGUE.

The wisest man who ever lived had much to say about the proper use of the tongue. He knew that if it was controlled, it can glorify God. If not, it serves Satan. I am including here some of the most beautiful references which Solomon made to the tongue and its value.

"The tongue of the righteous is as choice silver" (Proverbs 10:20). This is an excellent example of the treasure which those who belong to God can be storing up for themselves in heaven.

"He that uttereth truth showeth forth righteousness; but a false witness, deceit. There is one that speaketh rashly like the piercing of a sword; but the tongue of the wise is health" (Proverbs 12:17, 18). Those who speak the truth will reveal their basic nature of good. We also see how painful rash words can be and how healing and kind is the wise speech.

"A gentle tongue is a tree of life" (Proverbs 15:4). Part of the abundant life promised by Christ will be found in the gentle use of the tongue. For truly nothing has more effect on the life we lead than the words of our mouth.

"Whoso keepeth his mouth and his tongue keepeth his soul from troubles" (Proverbs 21:23). Surely we can understand that a lot of our earthly troubles are a direct result of not controlling our mouth. But even more important is the fact that many of our spiritual difficulties spring from the same source. Bridling the tongue can save us a lot of grief and heartache in this world and can serve to justify us for eternity with God.

"She openeth her mouth with wisdom; and the law of kindness is on her tongue" (Proverbs 31:26). The beautiful picture of the worthy woman exemplifies the value of wisdom in control of the tongue and a general attitude of kindness in the use of words. What a shame that so many Christian women can fulfill the other qualities of such a woman and fail on this one point!

THE NEW TESTAMENT ALSO CONTAINS ADMONITIONS CONCERNING THE TONGUE. We do not have to rely solely upon the Old Testament for principles and commands concerning our tongue. Christ realized the importance of this body organ and the problem it can cause and gives us help in our battle with it. The class may want to list all these for further study but at this time I am taking just one of them to illustrate the positive aspects of Christian speech.

"Let your speech be always with grace, seasoned with salt, that ye may know how to answer each one" (Colossians 4:6). This one verse is a "thumbnail" view of what our speech should be.

"ALWAYS WITH GRACE." This means we will use the right word at the right time. What a magnificent virtue this is! To be able to know just what to say when the occasion demands it. Our words will be truthful, courteous, dignified, wholesome and kind. If our conversation can pass the tests, we can be assured of letting it pass into the world.

"SEASONED WITH SALT." This is an odd comparison to use for words. And if we took only a modern day meaning of "salty," we would find it difficult to see why God chose this particular term to use in picturing Christian speech. A deeper study of salt however will bring out the more likely intention. First, salt is a seasoning; without it food is most tasteless. This would indicate that the Christian's words will be interesting, up to date and useful. True salt is a pure chemical and not a mixture. Therefore, our speech will be pure, not mixed with diluting worldliness. Second, salt is a preservative. This would mean that our conversation is lasting and of value. What we say will "keep" much as food preserved with salt kept its freshness for indefinite periods. People can trust that what we say will be as acceptable and valid in the future as at the time we speak. Third, salt is antiseptic. Before the advent of modern medicines, salt was used in many healing processes. Thus, our speech should have a positive influence on our listeners. It will not cut or otherwise wound, but will serve to heal the spiritual ills of the world.

The ability to speak is truly a marvelous gift from God. When it is used to its fullest potential for good, it will serve Him in honor and glory. A wisely controlled tongue can do much to insure the abundant life and its wonderful relationship with loved ones and fellow Christians. Love will help us use our words in the proper way, so let us pray that we can be guided by this lasting, eternal asset in the Christian life.

Let our attitude toward others' speech be as this expressed by an unknown writer, "Oh, the comfort, the inexpressible comfort, of feeling safe with a person; having neither to weigh thoughts nor measure words, but pouring them all right out, just as they are, chaff and grain together; certain that a faithful hand will take and sift them, keep what is worth keeping and with a breath of kindness, blow the rest away."

TO THINK UPON

1. Have someone make a chart of Bible references to the use of the tongue—good and bad—and present it to the class.

2. Discuss other causes for sins of the tongue which we did not list.

3. Why do you feel women have more trouble controlling their tongues than men?

4. How can our speech "betray" what kind of person we are?

5. Discuss immodest, impatient and indiscreet speech and give examples of each.

CHAPTER VII

"CHRISTIANITY IS GOOD MENTAL HEALTH"

The modern world is moving at an accelerated pace. And with the passing of each day, it seems to pick up even more speed. This naturally causes many problems and difficulties when man tries to adjust himself to the way of life which he has to face. Countless numbers are not able to cope with this life and its perplexities. Our hospitals are full of those whose emotions were not able to meet the challenges of daily living and thus, brought about breakdowns. As a direct result of this inability to cope with life, a whole new field of medical science has developed. You read of it most every time you pick up a newspaper or magazine and you hear it discussed on radio and television. Think now! When was the last time you heard or read something concerning **Mental Health?**

Man has come to understand that the mental part of his being is of vital importance. His physical health may be excellent but unless his mental health is satisfactory, he cannot actively and fruitfully engage in living a full, rich life. A scientific term for mental health is "psychological equilibrium." When a person is mentally healthy we understand that he is doing a good job of maintaining a balance among the inside and outside forces which affect every area of his life.

A recent article reported the findings of the Menninger Foundation, one of the most reputable of our mental research groups. The fourteen senior members of this Foundation were asked to describe a person who was mentally healthy. The resulting specifications were tabulated and the conclusions published. These men reported that mentally healthy people behave consistently in six important ways. I read this information over several times and with each study I began to feel more positive that these six characteristics were all based on Bible truths! Man feels he is discovering new principles every day and the findings of these so-called discoveries are published regularly. Actually he has failed to go back to the source of all things and in ignoring God's word, his findings are mere human repetition of precepts taught from the beginning by the One who created everything.

We will take a closer look at the six characteristics of the mentally healthy person as set forth by the Menninger Foundation and see where they find their basic truths in the Bible.

THE MENTALLY HEALTHY PERSON HAS A WIDE VARIETY OF SOURCES OF GRATIFICATION. This means he will be interested in a number of things and will find pleasure in many different people and ways. This ability enables him to sustain himself in case he loses one or more sources of gratification. For example, if a person has only one friend and he loses that friend, where can he turn for comfort? Thus, to have many friends insures him against such utter bereavement. If a person enjoys only one interest in life and something occurs which would physically hinder him from participating in that pleasure, he will naturally turn inward in self-pity. To enjoy many things will serve to fill his life if one activity is denied him. His personality is well-rounded because it is not limited to a single interest.

Do we find evidence of this quality in the Bible? I believe we do. Paul, in I Corinthians 9:22 said that he became "all things to all men in order that some might be won." Now if we say that Paul was not interested in the things he had to participate in to win others, we are placing him in the role of a hypocrite. Of course we know he was not this. I believe that Paul took pleasure in the things he used in trying to teach these people. They were not the most important interests in his life, but he could still enjoy them. It had to be a genuine concern or else his associates would have sensed the insincerity and sham of a "put on" interest.

The work of the church lends itself to this variety of interests very well. It has been concluded that this work falls into four basic categories—worship, exhortation, edification and benevolence. It is the responsibility of every Christian to participate in each facet of the functions of the body of Christ. And to participate to the best of our ability will mean that we have an interest in each area. To worship acceptably carries with it the duty to be concerned with the spiritual and its glory and exaltation. If we try to teach the gospel to those in the world, we must take an active concern in their interests if we are to be successful. A teacher who is superior in her work will be the one who is trying to understand her pupils, their lives and their interests. If she can have a part with them, she will more readily have access to their attention in order to present Christ to them. Last, the benevolent work of the church should be carried out by those people who have an empathetic understanding of those being helped. Varied sources of interest and gratification? Certainly there is Bible principle behind that facet of mental health.

THE MENTALLY HEALTHY PERSON IS FLEXIBLE UNDER STRESS. This means that they can "roll with the punches." Their problems are still there but they have the ability to cope with them, conquer them or live with them as the occasion demands. This should be the picture of Christians if they have the faith to believe what God has promised. "In nothing be anxious; but in everything by prayer and supplication with thanksgiving let your requests be made known unto God. And the peace of God, which passeth all understanding, shall guard your hearts and your thoughts in Christ Jesus" (Philippians 4:6, 7). This is as much a command as those which require baptism, yet how many of us miss this wonderful peace by not taking advantage of this sure promise?

"But God is faithful, who will not suffer you to be tempted above that ye are able; but will with the temptation make also the way of escape, **that ye may be able to endure it**" (I Corinthians 10:13). For years I took this to mean that God would provide a way of freedom from every temptation. But with some temptations I did not get this release and I was frustrated. How joyful I was when I finally read the latter part of this verse! There are some temptations and difficulties which will not be taken from us; these we must live with. The way of escape promised is the ability to bear them! What a difference this can make in our life!

Finally, we have the absolute assurance that **anything** which might happen to us will fit together in a pattern for good in our life. "And we know that to them that love God all things work together for good . . . " (Romans 8:28). No wonder the Christian can be flexible under stress. He has the promise of all the power he needs to strengthen him for such duress.

THE MENTALLY HEALTHY PERSON WILL RECOGNIZE THEIR LIMITATIONS AND THEIR ASSETS. The Menninger report puts it this way, "They have a reasonably accurate picture of themselves and they accept what they see. This does not mean they are complacent about themselves, but that they know they cannot be anyone else, and that is all right with them." This attitude should be a distinct feature of the Christian life. The parable of the talents teaches us that everyone has at least one ability. And if we are a one-talented person, we must be faithful stewards of that single unit just as if we had five! How can you be faithful if you do not have the proper respect for what you can accomplish?

All the exhortations to "examine yourselves" and "take heed to yourselves" are given with the idea that such examination will lead you to accept what you are and how you can use it in the service of God and fellow man. The Christian has no reason to feel unequal to the task before him because he has access to the greatest source of power in all the world and beyond. Paul knew this when he said that he could do "all things through Christ which strengtheneth me." The child of God knows and accepts that within himself he is nothing, yet at the same time he has all confidence that God is able to work within him to do His will and pleasure with the assets which He has granted to each. No reason for inferiority complexes here!

THE MENTALLY HEALTHY PERSON WILL TREAT OTHER PEOPLE AS INDIVIDUALS. This means that he will not be completely preoccupied with himself. If he is, he will pay only superficial attention to others for he will tend to lump all people into one category and place himself in another. The mentally healthy person is not so tied up with his own feelings that he does not care about the concerns and problems of others. He really looks at them as separate individuals and heeds their needs as he does his own.

Philippians 2:4 exhorts us to look not to our own things but "each of you also to the things of others." The very heart of Christianity is love. And love does not place all humanity in one group but rather seeks each as a separate entity, looking out its interests, problems and needs. The Christian truly is "not an island." His life is bound up with many individual relationships and he accepts each on its own merits. Christ was concerned with the individual; He made His plea to every person to "Come." It was not issued to groups of people or any organization but was a clarion call to the individual to form a relationship with his Savior. The followers of Christ cannot reject this example but must look to the importance of each person as a complete being within himself. For each possesses a distinct and unique soul unlike any other and should be treated accordingly.

THE MENTALLY HEALTHY PERSON IS ACTIVE AND PRODUCTIVE. This person will use his abilities and resources in his own behalf and in behalf of others. They do what they do because they enjoy it and appreciate their skills which enable them to do so. They are happy to be used in any capacity in which they are able to serve. Again, this is an accurate picture of the Christian, for they are part of a "going" and "doing" religion. Every book of the New Testament is filled with the activities of Christians busy in the service of the Lord. Also of the fruits produced by their action! The life which we are to live as children of God is not passive nor stagnant. We are challenged to be a living, vital testimony of our Savior. The proof of our success in this endeavor is the same as in the world of nature. If a plant is to be profitable, it must bear fruit. The Christian who does not produce will suffer the same fate as the sterile plant. But there is no need for anxiety on the part of the Christian for God will see that they can be "complete, furnished thoroughly unto every good work" (II Timothy 3:17).

THE MENTALLY HEALTHY PERSON WILL HAVE GOALS IN LIFE. They are not involved in an aimless, drifting existence. They look toward their ideals and strive to make them reality. The Christian has the same admonition in Matthew 6:33. "Seek ye first his kingdom, and his righteousness; and all these things shall be added to you." This is our primary goal in life and when it has its rightful place then all other secondary goals will fit in successfully. Paul looked toward a goal also and urged us to keep our eyes on that which is ahead instead of looking back. Once we have set our feet on the "narrow way" then we can continue toward our goal. And the life we then live will be as though we have "wings as an eagle." Our goal is an eternal life in heaven but seeking that goal actively will produce the abundant life promised by Christ.

To heed the principles of the New Testament is to be not only a Christian, but a mentally healthy person as well. Surely this is what God intended for His children here on earth. Let us now seek some ways in which we can implement these characteristics in our life. These will be as practical as possible so that they might be the most help in having good mental health.

1. START WITH A SELF-EVALUATION. But not the usual self examination! Rather set down on paper all your good points—honestly. Ignore the "I am nots" and the "I don't" and be positive. Put down all the "I ams" and "I cans." Then make a list of the qualities you would most like to add to these other virtues. Now start working toward achieving them!

2. RESPOND TO SITUATIONS INSTEAD OF REACTING. As human beings we tend to "react" to situations of life rather than respond. Responding means that we will notice the little things—the beauty of the color of life all around us which we often miss by looking at it as a big picture. Life is actually small views knit together to make a whole. We see the complete picture and react because of the general impressions we get. Learn to respond to the depth behind the big scene. Look around you at this very instant and see just how much beauty you can see in the small things surrounding your position. You'll find you've been ignoring most of the glory of life. For example: is that a wee spider crawling up the curtain? What is your impulse? Probably you react instinctively to brush it off and step on it. Wait a minute! Stop and really respond to that tiny creature. Look at its perfectness and yes, even its beauty. Is it really harming anything by wending its way up your drapery? Perhaps it is on its way to visit a friend or to find some food. Why not leave it be? And what is that you have in your pocket, Johnny? Oh, just some rocks I picked up. Again, do we react or respond? Take a look at the rocks; see them through Johnny's eyes. See, they do have a beauty all their own. Now, I'm not telling you that you must let spiders over-run your home or that your child should be allowed to carry rocks into the house. What you do with the situation after you respond to it is up to you as individuals. You might catch the insect and put it outside. Or you can wash the rocks and set them on Johnny's dresser (and later discard them). But I urge you to take a minute and respond to life instead of our usual negative reaction.

3. YIELD GRACEFULLY TO OTHERS. Be magnanimous toward the opinions and foibles of our fellow man. We are sometimes so set in

our ways we cannot accept the value of another's ideas. Start by letting someone else have his way today!

4. LEARN TO "UNLEARN." Prejudice is the key which locks the door to many opportunities of new learning. We think we know something and we are not willing to investigate any other possibility. Develop the attitude of listening and comparing what you know to what you hear and read. As parents this is an especially valuable asset because the knowledge we learned in our schooldays is becoming more obsolete by the hour. Our mind should be opened to new interests, new people and new knowledge, even if it means discarding some of our time-worn prejudices and gems of understanding.

5. LEARN TO ACT YOUR AGE AND ENJOY IT. This is true whether you are a teenager, young adult, middle aged or in the golden years. For you, the best age is what you are at the moment. It has to be for you cannot turn the pages to the past nor can you jump into the future. There is something wonderful, special and good about each distinct year and we should learn to accept every passing age as the best, looking forward to the next one as the best yet!

6. LEARN TO ENJOY OTHERS. People know whether you really like them. Their attitude toward you will be judged accordingly. Lincoln once said, "I don't like that man; I must get to know him better." How often we prejudge someone and then after we come to know him, find he is not so bad after all! Perhaps this is why Lincoln could say, "I never met a man I didn't like." Each person has something to offer your life; look for that good and make it a part of your relationship.

7. COLLECT LIKES—DISCARD DISLIKES. The Christian life should be one of aggressively collecting positives. When we find something we do not like about another, we should discard that immediately. Then we should set about finding things about them which we do like. If this is followed, I can guarantee that your circle of friends will grow and you will be a happier, contented person.

8. DEVELOP AN "ITCHING MIND." There is so much to learn in this world of ours. The library is full of books which we can read. There are lectures at many adult education centers. Even television offers home study courses. The mentally healthy person will keep that "itch" in his intellect, constantly "scratching" it with some new thought, some new study, some new book.

9. REALIZE THAT WE ARE OUR OWN WORST ENEMIES. No one can cheat or deceive or defeat us like we ourselves. It has been truthfully said that "no one can make you feel inferior unless you yourself cooperate."

Learn to think positively about yourself and your abilities. Proper self-love will gain us a new and best friend—ourself!

10. HAVE COURAGE. It takes many things to live the Christian life and one of the most important is courage. Boldness in accepting the challenges before us will make us face up and move ahead. Fear will make us run, hide or stand still. Christ comforted His followers and told them to be of good courage. He also promised to be with them always, "even to the end of the world." That promise is just as valid today!

FEAR IS AN ENEMY OF GOOD MENTAL HEALTH. An attitude of fearfulness causes more things to be left undone than any other thing. In our fast-paced world, we sometimes feel insecure and that breeds more fear. But the same admonition to be of good courage stretches forth from the pages of the New Testament and helps us battle this enemy of both our physical and spiritual life. We are most often afraid of things not revealed and sometimes when they come to light, we can see how foolish we were to be concerned. There are many areas of fearfulness in women today. We cannot cover them all but here are several. By bringing them out in'the open perhaps we can dispel our fear.

1. WE RIDE THE FENCE TOO MUCH. We are afraid to take a position and stand firm. Notice that I said **position** and not opinion. We cannot make up our minds therefore we are swayed by every wind of theory that blows by. Pontius Pilate was afflicted with this difficulty. He could not make up his mind and kept trying to place his responsibility in other hands. There is no neutral ground in living the Christian life. Our choice is either for God's way or the way of the world—no place on a fence which does not really exist.

2. WE ARE AFRAID TO BEGIN BECAUSE WE ARE AFRAID TO FAIL. So we miss many opportunities because we fear that we cannot accomplish the things necessary to accept them. In the first place, we depend too much on self. God's help is ours and always ready, but this power is not miraculous. It comes only with our active seeking and desiring to use it for the glory of our Father. We must accept the fact that we will fail sometimes, but we should not lose courage when this happens. We "forget that which is behind" and push forward to the next opportunity where we won't fail. Optimism will aid us in utilizing the power of God's help in achieving great things in our life.

3. WE ARE AFRAID OF OUR LIMITATIONS SO WE FAIL TO USE WHAT WE HAVE. The parable of the talents points this out quite vividly. The one-talent steward was afraid to use what he had been given so he hid it instead. The result? It was taken from him. I can guarantee that if we accept the responsibility of what we **can** do, they will be in-

creased as time goes by. Read that parable again and see if this is not true. We try to measure ourselves against some other's abilities and when we do not make the grade, we run and hide, giving excuses why we can't accept some task. The greatest source of unused power in the church today is the "hidden" talents of fearful Christian stewards.

4. WE FEAR LONELINESS. Loneliness can be a dreadful thing. It can effect a person in solitude and it can touch one in the midst of a great throng. The Christian need never be lonely for God is ever at hand. David was admonished, "Be still and know that I am God." How often could we heed this also and dispel the desolate feelings which overwhelm us. Our spiritual being can literally reach out and take the hand of God and who can be lonely with God as a companion?

There is a great difference between being lonely and being alone. Every person needs a time of aloneness. Seeking a period of solitude and quietness can serve to recharge our spiritual batteries and bring us closer to God and thus, closer to our earthly relationships.

5. WE FEAR DESPONDENCY. This dejection can eat away at us until we become extremely difficult to live with. This attitude plagues so many Christian women and is caused by many things. We grow despairing over the routine sameness of our life. Well, this is our own fault. There is no reason why our household chores have to be done in exactly the same manner at exactly the same time each day. Perhaps we could vary it by changing our schedule a bit. We can always let our mind "soar" outward when we are working at such menial tasks as sweeping, doing the dishes and ironing. I have discovered a valuable time for prayer in my own routine. I found that while I am vacuuming, my mind can reach out to God and I spend this time in prayer. The job does not take mental attention and the sound of the motor shuts out all outside noises and distractions. I center my mind and my thoughts on petitions to Him and have learned to be grateful for this new-found time of communion.

Women often become despondent over growing old. This is almost unique with the female because not many men are concerned with advancing age. Perhaps we feel this way because the world tends to gear everything for the young and we feel that everything is passing us by. This is really a matter of attitude for life is what each person makes it. An old maxim states "Live so that life seems like it will go on forever." The abundant life of the Christian accepts each day with the idea of filling it as full as we are able. Age might slow us down a bit physically but our mind and attitude is as young as spring! A beautiful older woman was described in this way, "As she grows older, she gets more beautiful inside and that's what counts!" Wrinkles may come on the outside but our inner being can be as fresh and beautiful as a young maiden. And that's what counts!

Let me suggest two hints which can help us keep in good mental health and live the abundant life without becoming frustrated and despondent. First, learn to say "No" if you can't do the best job because of other tasks you have. Complete each job you accept. And do not spread yourself so thin. It is better to say "no" than to accept and do a half-hearted, inadequate job. Second, reconsider how fast you're moving. If you are too busy, seek a slowing down. Let there be quiet times in your life. After all, under the many activities, you are a person with needs and problems. Better to respect yourself and heed the call to ease off a bit than to wind up with mental exhaustion.

Finally take a new look at God's world. It is truly a laboratory for living and we can learn much from it. Take the oyster for instance. A grain of sand irritates him, but he makes a pearl of it!

The Art of Achievement

By WILFERD A. PETERSON

You hold in your hand the camel's hair brush of a painter of Life. You stand before the vast white canvas of Time. The paints are your thoughts, emotions and deeds. YOU select the colors of your thoughts: drab or bright, weak or strong, good or bad. YOU select the colors of your emotions: discordant or harmonious, harsh or quiet, weak or strong. YOU select the colors of your deeds: cold or warm, fearful or daring, small or big. Through the power of your creative imagination you catch a vision . . . you dream a dream. YOU visualize yourself as the person you want to be. YOU see yourself as a builder, making a creative contribution to modern civilization. YOU strive to make the ideal in your mind become a reality on the canvas of Time. YOU select and mix the positive colors of heart, mind and spirit into the qualities of effective living, determination, endurance, self-discipline, work, love and faith. Each moment of your life is a brush stroke in the painting of your life. There are the bold, sweeping strokes of an increasing, dynamic purpose. There are the little touches that add the stamp of character and worth. There are the lights and shadows that make your life deep and strong. The art of achievement is the art of making life . . . your life . . . a MASTERPIECE!

TO THINK UPON

1. Why are mental problems so much harder to diagnose and treat than physical problems?

2. Have someone in the class read Carnegie's "How to Win Friends and

Influence People." See how many Bible principles are revealed in it.

3. List some of the interests outside the home in which Christian women can safely participate.

4. How can we best treat another as an individual?

5. Discuss why you feel there is no neutral ground in the Christian choice of life. (Or perhaps you feel there is. Discuss this.)

CHAPTER VIII

"WHAT IS THAT IN THINE HAND?"

History is a fascinating subject for only in it can the little people of the world walk arm and arm with the great men of the past. Only in it can we peep through a keyhole, so to speak, and behold their lives. In its pages we can attend conferences and secret meetings where weighty decisions were made that affected the course of nations. Only in history can we delve into the problems and solutions to questions which have encompassed mankind throughout the entirety of his existence upon the earth. Yet only as we use history as a schoolmaster can we hope to profit from the past, mold the present, and secure the future.

Bible history is no different, except that it is the only true history. It is not a fable or a myth which proved wrong as some secular history tales have. In the pages of the Bible we study about people—good and bad and even mediocre—and we look at the pictures of nations as they try to live together. The more we examine the past, the more conscious we are made of the similarities between the people of 6,000 years ago and those living today. Problems are alike; responses to these problems compare; and hate, love, joy, sorrow, the desire for material things, success and failure were very real parts of living then as they are now.

There were juvenile problems then. With the first two young people on earth we find jealousy erupting into murder. And the story of the prodigal son certainly exhibits the same lessons of rebellious, headstrong youth thinking itself to be wiser than its parents. The people of the past had family problems also. The twins, Jacob and Esau, were involved in difficulties akin to the ones we find today when a parent shows partiality to one child. Take a look at Jacob and his traveling household of wives and children! If ever people were caught up in family problems, here was a group with built-in dilemmas.

There was disobedience and obedience. There was war and peace. There were times of depression and times of prosperity. Nothing much has really changed except the way we dress, the way we travel, and our faster pace of living. People in days gone by have been tempted to quit when problems loomed larger and larger. Some did—others did not! The purpose of this lesson is to picture the many ways which we can qualify and the things we can utilize in living the Christian life. No one likes a quitter; but a qualifier is always respected.

First, let's look at some Bible examples of quitters and qualifiers:

ADAM AND EVE were quitters. They started out good, made a mistake and then quit. JONAH tried to run away. He quit before he even started. Yet through the grace of God, he was later allowed to qualify. ELIJAH tried to sit down and quit. Jezebel had run him out of the country. He hid in a cave, pouting and ready to quit because there were four hundred prophets of Baal to himself. Odds of 400 to 1 seem quite large until you realize that God was on the side of the one! God did not let Elijah quit but told him to get up and qualify for the job He had for him to do. JEREMIAH gave up when he thought he was the only one left. MOSES AND GIDEON were ready to quit before they tried, but they went ahead and tried and qualified. DAVID could have quit after his mistake with Bathsheba. MARY MAGDALENE could have quit in shame because of her past. MATTHEW was a despised tax collector but he didn't quit!

PAUL was a quitter in a sense and we read to learn this positive lesson from his quitting. He **quit** the evil he was doing and qualified for the good. NICODEMUS was wealthy and could have quit because following Jesus was unpopular. Yet he was there when they prepared Jesus' body for the tomb. JUDAS quit.

Of course we know these are only a few of the lessons we can learn from God's word about people who either drifted through life emptily or who utilized time and effort to present a successful life to their God. But whether we look at these from the past or those living around us today, we can recognize certain characteristics which all "quitters" possess.

1. QUITTERS TALK ABOUT PEOPLE INSTEAD OF THINGS. Through some odd quirk of their mind, these people seem to think that they elevate their own position by running down someone else. They are so busy finding things to say about other people that their mind stagnates into a receptacle of gossip and unworthy thoughts.

2. QUITTERS ARE ALWAYS LOOKING FOR THE EASY WAY. Whether it is in house work or finding the way to heaven, the quitter wants to find a short-cut around the necessary requirements. They don't want to spend the time and effort it takes to present a first-class household to the world or an acceptable life to God.

3. QUITTERS YIELD TO THE MATERIAL THINGS OF LIFE. They let material possessions have complete emphasis in their life. They do not have the faith to look beyond that which they can see, hear, feel, taste or touch. Everything must be "proved" to them before they will accept it as a fact.

4. QUITTERS ARE MENTALLY LAZY. Instead of trying to qualify for any work, they make excuses. They say they have no education, no money, no background and never had much chance in life. They have no valid reasons for their indolence; but an excuse is ever ready on their

lips. An elderly minister once gave me some good advice concerning excuses. He said, "Don't ever make excuses. In the first place, your friends don't need them because they love you and accept you for what you are. In the second place, your enemies won't heed them. So why waste the time and effort?"

5. QUITTERS RUN ON EMOTION. They show little self-control and discipline. Their life is marked by constant pouting, bickering and complaining. Their emotions control their actions and words instead of allowing good Christian judgment to hold sway.

6. QUITTERS ARE PESSIMISTIC. These people do not really know how to enjoy life because they are always looking at the ugly, negative side. They have artificial values because they do not have the faith to reach out for the more positive qualities promised by God. They feel that Christianity is an apologetic religion and try to make as many apologies about their involvement as they possibly can.

I am so grateful that history shows us the qualifiers as well as the quitters. A study of them will prove their qualities are worthwhile and well within our own reach today.

1. QUALIFIERS ARE TRUTH SEEKERS. They are never satisfied with their knowledge but keep an "itching" mind so they may constantly be increasing their learning. If they are shown new truths, they are eager and willing to accept them. If they can't find an answer, they are not too proud to ask help from someone older or wiser.

2. QUALIFIERS BASE CONCLUSIONS ON FACTS. They possess emotions, certainly but their decisions of life are not based on such flimsy foundation. Nor do they allow petty prejudice to control their thoughts. They seek to find the facts of a matter and then will act accordingly.

3. QUALIFIERS ARE OPTIMISTIC. They know the power of God's word and its ability to work within them. They are positive that the world would accept the Truth if it only knew what it was. Therefore they spend their time in finding ways to reveal the Truth to others. They believe the gospel is truly good news and they speak of it in that enthusiastic manner. They have the faith to tackle a new job with the attitude of "With God's help, I know I can."

4. QUALIFIERS USE MATERIAL BLESSINGS WELL. They know that these were given them by a gracious God and they find ways to enjoy them and to turn that enjoyment into a service to the One who provided them. They appreciate the beauties of nature, as well as the man-made conveniences. Yet they never lose the awareness of where these came from and how they should use them.

5. QUALIFIERS ARE SELF-DISCIPLINED. Every area of their life exhibits this quality of self-control. They are not afraid to work and never offer excuses for failing. Their labor produces quality evidence whether it is at home, school, civic functions, work, or in the service of God.

6. QUALIFIERS HAVE A FORWARD LOOK. They know they are running a race and cannot afford to look back nor to the side. Their eyes are on their goal and all their actions are centered on achieving their aim of an abundant life here on earth and eternity in heaven with their Savior.

Paul often compared the Christian life with a race and we can see the similarity between the two. Whether it be a physical competition or the spiritual contest, there are certain rules which must be followed by those who participate.

1. We must know the rules and be willing to abide by them. In the Christian endeavor this is accomplished by daily study of God's word wherein are found the rules for our competition.

2. We must prepare ourself to be healthy and vigorous for the task. The Christian keeps his physical and spiritual bodies healthy to enable him to serve well and acceptably in the Lord's work.

3. We must be willing to put forth the effort. God will not save anyone who does not fulfill his share of the bargain. Living the Christian life is not a "bed of roses." It takes time, thought and physical and spiritual effort to run the race successfully.

4. We must have the heart to win—in other words, the winning spirit. Any other spirit in running this race will only hinder the competitor from reaching his fullest potential. This positive desire for the prize offered, coupled with a love for the One offering it, should spur the Christian to a better race.

5. We must not quit. Naturally the winner must conclude the race. He cannot start, tire, lag behind and finally stop. He must put forth every effort until the finish line is crossed.

How can we better run the Christian race today? How can we be qualifiers instead of quitters? For this, I want to go back to another Bible example:

Moses had fled from Egypt in great fear. Now for forty years he had led the quiet, peaceful, uneventful life of a shepherd. But all this is about to come to an end. He stands before a bush which, though burning furiously, is not consumed. From that burning bush, God tells Moses that he must go back to Egypt and bring His people out of bondage. Moses is not eager to accept this mission and begins to give excuses as to why he can't do what God wants. (He wants to quit before he even tries to qualify!) But God was not interested in excuses then— and neither is He today—and to show Moses that He didn't expect him to tackle this job alone, He asked, "Moses, what is that in thine hand?"

Moses looked down and saw only his shepherd's staff. But God saw something else and told him to cast it down on the ground. Immediately that rod became a snake! When God told Moses to pick it up, it became the staff again. Moses could see only a utilitarian object but God knew He could make it a thing of power.

This presents a picture of so many Christian women today. We are standing before God's voice in His word and giving excuses. God might very well ask of us, "What is that in thine hand?" And none of us are empty-handed. We might see only every-day articles and abilities but perhaps God can see something else. With His power, anything we have at hand can serve to glorify Him in some way. So we are now going to ask ourself the question which God posed to Moses and see what varied answers we can find. I honestly believe each of us can find something in our hands useful in qualifying for the Christian race.

WHAT IS THAT IN THINE HAND?

I HAVE A WEDDING RING. Can this serve God? Yes. Being a godly wife is fulfilling the primary role which our Creator placed upon woman. When we follow the commands concerning this part of our life, we can be assured this will be reflected in the influence of our household. Our husbands can better serve God and we can more readily reach out to teach others if we are living up to God's standard as a wife. If our husband is not a Christian, being the right kind of mate could well lead him to the truth. Yes, a wedding band can certainly be used to glorify God.

I HAVE A LITTLE CHILD. I can use this also to serve God. First, it is the role of motherhood which gives us more influence over other lives, for these children come into our hands to be molded and shaped for a future earthly existence, as well as an eternal one. Being a godly mother will bring honor to Him who gave us the privilege of cooperating with Him in bringing a human being with an immortal soul into this world. I can teach Christian ideals and attitudes to my children by a constant awareness of the things around us which so aptly illustrate God's love and care for us—flowers, rain, all of nature, our family, and so much other. I can utilize for my own benefit some of the wonderful characteristics of my children—their forgiveness, their cheerfulness and above all, their explicit trust in their father. (If we as God's children could only have the same abiding confidence in our heavenly Father!)

Perhaps the greatest service with a little child is in preparing his soul for eternity. The mother has more influence on this pliable little life and it is her own care and teaching which so often leads the child to obey the gospel. Through her own children, perhaps she can reach their friends and playmates with the beauty of Christ by having Bible story sessions with cookies and Kool-Aid afterward. Sure it takes a little time, but use that which is within your hand!

I HAVE MY HOME. Hospitality is one of the greatest assets a Christian can possess. The possibilities of using the home in the work of the church are almost unlimited. We can have parties for our Christian and non-Christian friends to show that religion does not have to be a down-in-the-mouth way of life. We can let them see that Christian fellowship is rich and enjoyable, without all the drinking and dancing which characterizes worldly entertainment.

I can bring young people of the church into my home for clean, wholesome activities. Since we know there are certain things we must forbid them, we should make certain they also realize that these are not necessary to have fun. If we provide nothing positive for those negative things we object to, then we have no reason to be surprised when they seek questionable actions and places to fill their time.

We can also use our home for having visiting teachers and preachers enjoy the fellowship of our family. Too many do this out of a sense of duty and those poor preachers usually know this. Opportunities of this sort can serve to widen our own horizons of knowledge and to help our children accept the values of good conversation with knowledgeable visitors.

I HAVE A BROOM. How can I serve God with this simple household object? I can make certain that my home is clean and cheerful. While the Bible does not state that "cleanliness is next to Godliness" there is much truth in the maxim. It has been proven that outside influence can affect the inward emotions. Then it would follow that a neat, orderly house would help more housewives have neat, orderly emotions! When the emotions are under control, life is much easier to face. Let's man that broom for God!

I HAVE SOME POTS AND PANS. How can these vessels serve to honor God? This is easy to see when we realize that a healthy body can better work in any capacity. Therefore to provide good, wholesome meals for my family is an excellent way to glorify God with my pots and pans. Since our body is the temple of the spirit, how better can a mother live the abundant life than to see those bodies nourished properly? If I have teenage children this is an especially difficult task. Surveys prove that this age group has the worst eating habits in the world. I can see that good, healthy snacks are provided and that mealtime has the best diet for these young bodies.

I can also make goodies for the older people in the neighborhood or in the congregation. Or perhaps we have some shut-ins who would appreciate some cookies or a cake? To take a needed meal to that family whose mother is in the hospital is a way to qualify in the Christian race also. I can bake something to take when I go visiting for the Lord. It is always nice to come "bearing gifts."

I HAVE A COMB AND BRUSH. Can **these** be used in the Christian race? Certainly! Good personal grooming habits can make one more acceptable to other people. I owe it to God to make the best of the natural gifts He has given me. But I can also use these objects in other ways. If I have a knack for fixing hair, I can have a group of young Christian girls in my home and help them learn how to present their best to the world. Many of them look the way they do simply because they do not know how to do better—and no one else has taken the time to help them. I can also take this ability to the hospital and help one who cannot set their own hair and to the bedfast home patient who would appreciate looking their best even when they do not feel it.

I HAVE A WASHING MACHINE AND IRONING BOARD. I can use these in the Christian life by first assuring my family of fresh, clean clothing when they need it. Especially will I have everything ready on Sunday morning so that preparing to go to worship will go smoothly and calmly, with no last minute rushing to iron a dress or shirt or dig a pair of needed socks from the dirty clothes hamper. Second, I can help other families in their emergency situations, when the mother has a new baby or when there is a death or illness in the home. Sometimes it is the most ordinary of tasks which make the best gift to others, and laundry is an excellent way of "giving yourself away."

I HAVE A SEWING MACHINE. Our best example for a Christian use of this appliance can be found in Acts 9 where the touching story of Dorcas is told. This godly woman was destined to be honored in God's inspired word and to be remembered for generations in the future simply because she was a seamstress and used that talent to the glory of God (and she did it all by hand!) I can provide garments for my own family and make clothing for the needy wherever they might be. This is a need which will never be completely filled and calls out for women to accept the responsibility and challenge to sew for the Lord's service.

I HAVE A TELEPHONE. Can this instrument be used to honor our Father? In some ways yes, but there is a great danger lurking in the possibilities offered by its use. I can call absentees, shut-ins, newcomers, the lonely and to organize a program of work. But I must be careful that it does not degenerate into a gossip machine, thereby devaluating any good I might otherwise do. Great care must be exercised in utilizing this convenience lest it control us instead of the other way around.

I HAVE A PENCIL OR PEN. These can be used to write letters to the lonely people who need our cheering. I can send a note to those who are ill; I can thank someone for a kindness or some service they render. I can write invitations to a gospel meeting or vacation Bible school. I can show appreciation for the visit of someone to our worship. There are many uses for these little tools we take so for granted. Why not try some of them today!

I HAVE AN AUTOMOBILE STEERING WHEEL. God has granted Americans many, many material blessings which can be used in His service. The automobile is one of these yet how often do we think of it only as a family convenience? It can take me visiting to the many people I should call on for the Lord. Surely there are others who need a ride to worship Sunday and Wednesday. Do I have an extra space in the car for them? I can bring women to ladies' class because many of them do not keep their family car during the day. When vacation Bible school time comes, I can fill my automobile with the children who dearly love to attend these worthwhile classes. Convenience? Yes, but our family car can be far more than that to God.

I HAVE ARTISTIC ABILITY. This God-given talent is sorely needed in God's work in every congregation I know of. Yet too often those blessed with this gift do not offer it in His service. It can be used in helping teachers with their class handwork or decorating their rooms. Young people's banquets can be truly beautiful with just the right artistic touches to the table favors and centerpieces. If you possess this wonderful ability, may I urge you to develop and collect ideas which can be placed in book form to be used throughout the brotherhood. There is such a need for material like this to help the teacher who, though sufficient in other areas, has no artistic feeling for handwork, decorations or other visual aids. This talent helps you see the beauty in life all around. Use it to aid others in seeing that same loveliness of form and color.

I HAVE A LIKING FOR SMALL CHILDREN AND THEY LIKE ME. Then you are badly needed in many areas of the Lord's work. Young mothers who would like to teach classes cannot do so because of their small children. Here is where you can help. Become a baby-sitter for God! Visitation programs, work day to help the needy, special training courses —all these need the loving care of a person who will tend the small children while their mothers participate. Giving her this relief could mean a happier wife and mother when the day draws to a close. It's just a little while of your time but it might be the "making" of her day.

I HAVE A LISTENING EAR. In a world so full of talk, talk, talk this quality is becoming quite rare. You can always find someone to make a speech but it's often hard to find someone to just listen. This is an extra special need for our older people because those of us who are younger no longer take the time to just sit and listen to them. What they have to say may be quite trivial or insignificant to us—but it is very important to them. Give your listening ear to some of these wonderful senior citizens. Another area where the listening ear is valuable is with our children. We should never become so busy we cannot give them that few minutes to tell what is on their mind. Perhaps they want to confide in us some small secret. How precious are these moments shared with another by listening! And what dividends they will pay when those little children grow into teenagers!

I HAVE THE ABILITY TO WRITE. When my first book was published in 1964, I had no idea what to expect as to its acceptance by the women of the church. I was overwhelmed at their eagerness and their wonderful kindness in using this work of mine. I do not flatter myself that it was because of any excellence in what I had written. It was merely because there is such a terrific need for material and Christian women are eager and ready to use all the study aids they can find. This is also true in all levels of Bible school, from the Toddlers up to the Adults. If you have the ability to write, use it to prepare lesson material for the church. Write articles for magazines and newspapers. Christians have only begun to find acceptance in the world of literature outside the church. With the sad state of books and writing in general, it is high time we should make the impact of moral literature felt on the public as a whole. We can, if enough Christians develop their ability to put their thoughts on paper.

I HAVE THE ABILITY TO SING. This is another talent which seems to go un-appreciated by its owner. Only those of us who can't "carry a tune in a bucket" know how very precious is this gift! To those of you who can sing, begin to use it in other ways than just worshipful singing during regular services. Start a children's chorus to help them develop an appreciation for God-approved music of our worship. Take this group to shut-ins, old folks' homes or even to the local shopping centers (with the permission of its managers, of course). Another great need is for a group to sing at weddings and funerals. It takes time, but this work can be so rewarding and needful. Use your talent to write songs for use in vacation Bible schools and other children's classes. With a song on your lips, you can encourage others in this Christian race of life.

I AM EMPLOYED OUTSIDE THE HOME. This, too, can be used to the glory of God. It means I will have a wider sphere of influence and have more opportunities to reach people with the Truth. They may never come in contact with another Christian life. I should remember that, even though another human being is my employer, my service is actually to God. My career is part of my spiritual life as much as attending worship on Sunday. I will be busy, keeping a job and a house too, but I must never be too busy to remember my influence on my fellow employees.

I HAVE THE BIBLE. This is our most valuable tool in running the Christian race. For from it we teach others the words which will grant them life everlasting and from it we learn the things we must do ourselves to finish this race acceptably. Women can be very effective in doing personal work. With our modern appliances giving us more free time, we should be preparing ourselves to teach others. I may fail with all the other things I hold in my hand but I must not fail with the Bible. It has power to touch and convict the hearts of those I present it to but only if it is given the opportunity to reach them. Hidden behind my back, away out of sight, the Bible still may be in my hand but I've taken it out of my heart! Keep it before you daily and use it diligently.

We have discussed only a few of things which we might find at hand if God were to ask us today. Surely, though, you can see that everyone has **something** in their hand which they can use to qualify in serving God. It is up to each of us to find our assets and use them to the best of our ability. We should take a good look at our talents in a completely honest manner. What am I best suited to do? Where do my interests lie? Can I learn to do anything new? It is natural that I can do best that which I know how or am interested in, but I should never miss an opportunity to learn other areas of service. Never feel too inadequate to accept the big jobs; and never feel too good to accept the small jobs.

Just Be The Best

If you can't be a pine on the top of the hill,
    Be a scrub in the valley — but be
The best little scrub at the side of the rill:
    Be a bush if you can't be a tree.
If you can't be a bush, be a bit of the grass
    Some highway to happier make;
If you can't be a muskie, then just be a bass
    But the liveliest bass in the lake.
We can't all be captains, we've got to be crew.
    There's something for all of us here;
There's big work to do and there's lesser to do,

And the task we must do is the near.
If you can't be a highway, then just be a trail;
  If you can't be a sun, be a star.
It isn't by size that you win or you fail—
    BE THE BEST OF WHATEVER YOU ARE!
                    By Douglas Wallock

TO THINK UPON

1. List some Bible examples of "quitters" and "qualifiers" not mentioned in our lesson.

2. Why do you feel that the basic part of man has changed little through the centuries?

3. Why is optimism so important in living the Christian life?

4. Discuss some of the excuses women use for not participating in more areas of church work open to them.

5. Can you think of other things "in your hand" which might be used in serving God?

CHAPTER IX

"PERSONAL WORK IS JUST THAT"

"No one whose life has been truly touched by Christ is free to leave the matter there; he must, as a consequence, extend the boon. If the enkindling fire (Luke 12:49) which Christ said He came to light has in any sense entered a soul, that person cannot rest until he lights as many fires as possible. In short, a person cannot be a Christian and avoid being an evangelist!"

These words were written by Elton Trueblood in his **Company of the Committed.** True, they were not divinely inspired but just as true is the fact that they are based on the very foundation of the Great Commission. God loved man enough to send His Son to earth to live, suffer and die as the perfect sacrifice. These acts of divine love granted man the blessed hope of eternal life in heaven. Any person who comes in contact with the blood of Christ, receives the cleansing of sins, and becomes a member of the church of Christ therefore has the obligation, actually the privilege, of leading others to the place where humanity touches the holy in receiving God's gift of grace.

How many of my Christian brethren would be shocked if they were told they are obliged to be an evangelist in heralding the good tidings of salvation to a world moving rapidly to the brink of death and destruction? "Why," they will say, "an evangelist is a person hired by the congregation to preach the word." But this is true in only the very limited meaning of the word. Just because we help support a local minister does not take the responsibility of being an evangelist **personally** from our shoulders. When Christ gave the Great Commission, He was speaking physically to a small group of His followers. Spiritually He was issuing the marching orders of the church to every individual Christian from that day until the end of time! We may not recognize this; we may even hide the fact from our troubled conscience; but it is a solid true statement and one that will judge every follower of Christ in that last day.

Personal work has been an active part of Christianity from the moment of the church's inception on the Day of Pentecost. Those exact words are not used in the New Testament, but the concept is taught throughout its pages. Many Christians have come to regard the terms "Personal Work" or "Personal Evangelism" as almost dirty words. When this subject is taught or preached from the pulpit, they have guilt feelings and because these are unpleasant to them, they urge the minister to "lay off." Of course, they are not honest enough to give the real reason behind their fear of this exhortation so they hide behind a cloak of pretense. "People in this area just can't be taught." Or "Everyone is doing their best to teach others." Or, "You must preach more on God's wonderful love for us instead of all this hell, fire and brimstone if we don't do personal work."

I think we can all agree that we need more sermons on God's love for us and our love for Him and our fellow man. But, how do you teach one without teaching also the necessity of sharing that love with those outside the circle of safety? Of all my disappointments in my Christian brethren, I am most heartsick about this all too prevalent idea of "Let George do it" when it comes to spreading the gospel. Most usually "George" is the preacher or some dedicated teacher who will accept the necessity of personal involvement. Whatever excuses are given, the need is there and the call to "go and teach" will still ring down to each individual Christian as long as God allows the world to stand. Ignoring it will only bring greater condemnation down on our heads.

When we became Christians, in the truest sense of the word, we were literally committing our lives to God. Yet by and large the greatest majority of Christians in the world have not accepted the fact that this commitment carries with it the direct necessity to become **involved** in the work of the church. Commitment without involvement is as useless as putting the car key in the ignition but failing to turn it on. In my travels around the country, however, I am grateful that I can see an awakening to this need of personal involvement in teaching others. It is still small but with the help of God, I feel it will continue to grow, until as Mid McKnight puts it, "Brethren, we can take this old world for Christ any time you are ready."

But it will not be done without PERSONAL WORK. There is no way of getting around it; no polite side-stepping of the issue. The church will not grow as God would have it until there is a general acceptance of the fact that teaching others is most effectively done on a personal basis. And let's face it, this also involves work. Personal work is just that—**personal** and **work**. The sooner we quit trying to make excuses and have the courage to face up to our individual responsibility in this challenge, then the sooner we will see congregations growing out of their buildings, missionaries increasing in every field, benevolent work abounding, and a constant stream of baptisms in all areas of this world. Too long we have accepted the growth of our congregation to be the number of Christians moving into our town and placing membership. This is a minor part of true growth; the heart of expansion can only be judged by the number of converts we have been able to bring to the Christian way of life. And, fellow Christians, these are won—not with ease and little effort—but with the "sweat and tears and prayers" of a personal working of one human being with another.

The purpose of this lesson is not to give a treatise on the need for doing personal work nor the methods we might use in accomplishing this evangelistic involvement for Christ. There are many excellent works already published by worthy Christian men for these purposes and I could add nothing to them. Therefore, I am going to stress the words **personal work** and the many factors involved in their meaning. Since all words in our language are composed of individual letters, I thought I would take this method of searching out some of the depths behind all that the term **personal work** means to us as children of God. Personal work is spelled: P-E-R-S-O-N-A-L W-O-R-K. Let's take a look at what each letter might stand for.

P stands for PRAYER. "For this cause we also, since the day we heard it, do not cease to pray and make request for you, that ye may be filled with the knowledge of his will in all spiritual wisdom and understanding" (Colossians 1:9).

Paul prayed that his Colossian brethren might be filled with the knowledge of God's will in their lives. Before we can start any program of teaching another person the Truth, we must seek God in prayer. We need to communicate with Him concerning our anxieties in this work of leading another and ask His help in letting that one know what His will is for their life. We cannot pray that God will forgive their sins outside of obedience, but we can earnestly seek His help in preparing their hearts to be receptive to our teaching. Prayer must be the constant companion of the Christian who involves himself in personal evangelism. From the start of the relationship with a lost soul, through the steps of leading that one to the Truth, down to the final act of submission to God's will —prayer must be fervent and earnest, and with the sure knowledge that God will hear and answer!

E stands for EXPERIENCE. "For everyone that partaketh of milk is without experience of the word of righteousness; for he is a babe" (Hebrews 5:13). "And God is able to make all grace abound unto you; that ye, having always all sufficiency in everything, may abound unto every good work" (II Corinthians 9:8).

The most common excuse for failing to do personal work is "I can't do it. I don't know how." And this after they have been members of the church for many years! We grant that most Christians have not had experience in this work. But the only way to remedy that is to get busy. Hebrews 5:13 gives the only valid reason for lack of experience and that is the new babe in Christ. Yet how strange that often it is these very "inexperienced in the word" Christians who are more eager in trying to win others for Christ! Some will say "I can't teach. Some people just don't have the ability." This is a weak excuse and serves to point out a deeper failure on the part of that individual.

Hebrews 5:12 indicates that with the passage of time, **every** Christian should be prepared to teach others. This shows, of course, that the Christian has the responsibility to be studying the word of God in order that as time goes by, he will be able to use his knowledge to tell others the gospel story. This scripture offers no comfort to the Christian seeking an excuse from getting involved in personal work.

We learn best by doing and with that doing comes the necessary experience to be proficient at our task. There are countless methods of doing this work and in one of them, each of us can find a way to get busy in gaining experience in this field of service for God.

R stands for REWARD. "Then shall the King say unto them on his right hand, Come, ye blessed of my Father, inherit the kingdom prepared for you from the foundation of the world" (Matthew 25:34). "Behold, I come quickly; and my reward is with me, to render to each man according as his work is" (Revelation 22:12).

There are many rewards for doing personal work, both here on earth and the final spiritual reward. First, we have the satisfaction of knowing that we are doing God's will in helping others find the way to salvation. Second, there is no accurate description of the blessing gained from watching another walk down the aisle, confess the Son, and be baptized into His Body. The glorious feeling of knowing that **you** helped save a soul from eternal damnation! The final recompense for the efforts we make in winning others will be granted on the day of judgment when our reward will be given us by our Father. How magnificent this prize will be is far beyond our imagination! To read a description of what heaven will be like is only to whet our appetite and spur our energies on to further efforts to make certain we have a part in that eternal city.

S stands for SIMPLICITY. Luke 8:5-15 relates the parable of the sower and the kinds of earth where his seed fell. This story gives an accurate picture of the true simplicity of presenting the gospel to the world around us. I Corinthians 15:1-4 also is a good passage in teaching others for herein is the heart of what the gospel is all about. Those who have great fear of teaching because of a lack of knowledge can study this passage and learn the meaning behind it and can be ready to help others obey the gospel. Simple, yes, but oh so powerful!

The more I study and work with the scriptures, the more I realize that much of its power lies in its very simplicity. This is also a logical proof of its divinity and inspiration because it can be understood by all. God said He was not willing that **any** should perish. Looking at the world around us, we can readily see that the greater number of people on this earth are not the educated, theological-minded intellect group. No, the mass is without formal learning with no grounding in theology or any other "ology." So when God stated He desired that all should be taught of Him, we can be assured that what we have to teach is simple enough for the masses to understand—and yet it also has enough "meat" to satisfy the intellectual curiosity of those who possess it. To be afraid of the depth of the Bible will only keep us from using the heart of it to teach others. We can utilize the simple part and that is, after all, the most essential knowledge because it tells us how we may obtain salvation. We can leave the meatier portions to those better qualified to build on our foundation of simplicity.

O stands for OPTIMISM. "Having confidence in thine obedience I write unto thee, knowing that thou wilt do even beyond what I say" (Philemon 21). "Being confident of this very thing, that he who began a good work in you will perfect it until the day of Jesus Christ" (Philippians 1:6).

These passages were not written by Paul to non-Christians concerning their obedience. Yet they teach a quality which every Christian could well emulate—that of optimism. Paul, in writing the master of the runaway slave, stated his confidence that this fellow-Christian would go the second mile in taking back his servant. Christianity is a religion of confidence and I am always surprised that more of its followers have not caught the spirit. When Paul wrote the Philippians he expressed his confidence not only in them, but in Christ also, knowing that the indwelling of Christ in their hearts would serve to keep them faithful to the end.

One of the most valuable assets of the personal evangelist is optimism. If we go with the idea that "they don't really want to hear what I'm going to say and they won't listen," our actions will usually reveal this apathy to the one we are trying to teach. Sure enough, they aren't interested! Our attitude should be one of assurance, realizing that we are carrying the most powerful thing in the world when we bring God's word to another. We must believe that it does have power and that it will touch the heart of this individual. Then with love backing this position, we just cannot fail!

N stands for NECESSITY. "But be ye doers of the word, and not hearers only, deluding your own selves" (James 1:22).

"Because I have called, and ye have refused; I have stretched out my hand, and no man regarded; but ye have set at nought all my counsel, and would none of my reproof; I also will laugh in the day of your calamity; I will mock when your fear cometh; when your fear cometh as a storm, and your calamity cometh on as a whirlwind; when distress and anguish come upon you. Then will they call upon me, but I will not answer. They will seek me diligently, but they shall not find me. For that they hated knowledge, and did not choose the fear of Jehovah. They would none of my counsel, they despised all my reproof. Therefore shall they eat of the fruit of their own way, and be filled with their own devices. For the backsliding of the simple shall slay them, and the careless ease of fools shall destroy them. But whoso hearkeneth unto me shall dwell securely, and shall be quiet without fear of evil" (Proverbs 1:24-33).

"Son of man, I made thee a watchman unto the house of Israel: therefore hear the word at my mouth, and give them warning from me. When I say unto the wicked, Thou shalt surely die; and thou givest him not warning, nor speakest to warn the wicked from his wicked way, to save his life; the same wicked man shall die in his iniquity; but his blood will I require at thy hand. Yet if thou warn the wicked, and he turn not from his wickedness, nor from his wicked way, he shall die in his iniquity; but thou has delivered thy soul" (Ezekiel 3:17-19).

These passages are warning enough of the dire necessity of reaching those souls outside the safety of Christ. The urgency is two-fold: to save the lost from eternal destruction and to prove ourselves worthy in the service of God.

A stands for ATTITUDE. "And the servant of the Lord must not strive, but be gentle towards all, apt to teach, forbearing, in meekness correcting them that oppose themselves; if peradventure God may give them repentance unto the knowledge of the truth, and they may recover themselves out of the snare of the devil" (II Timothy 2:24-26).

This admonition of Paul to young Timothy should be the motto of every Christian involved in personal evangelism. It is frightening to think of how many arguments have been won at the expense of losing valuable souls. Brother Cloys Cecil of Minneapolis said a professor once asked him, "Why is it that so many church of Christ members come to me with arguments on their lips but none of Christ in their hearts?" This belligerent attitude of so many of us has closed numerous doors which never will be opened again. To teach others we must be gentle and forbearing, rather than trying to "cram the Truth down their throats." We do not have to tear down their religious beliefs. If we help them build a strong house of true faith, the old structure will tumble of its own accord. It is sad to see the sometimes arrogant feeling of Christians who know they possess the Truth, and if others want it, let them ask! Paul's advice to Timothy included the meek correction of error because God knew that those outside the church are in reality "opposing themselves." They do not understand what is best for them until they come to a knowledge of God's will for their salvation. I urge each of you to memorize this passage and commit it to your store of knowledge in working with the lost.

L stands for LOVE. "A new commandment I give unto you, that ye love one another; even as I have loved you, that ye also love one another. By this shall all men know that ye are my disciples, if ye have love one to another" (John 13:34, 35). "Beloved, let us love one another: for love is of God; and everyone that loveth is begotten of God, and knoweth God. He that loveth not knoweth not God; for God is love" (I John 4:7, 8).

If the Christian does not have love for his fellow man, he will never have real success as a personal worker. For how can you be concerned about another's soul if you don't care what happens to that person? Perhaps this is the actual reason why so many Christians are doing nothing to win souls to Christ. Can it be that we do not possess enough love for those outside His Body—that we just do not care enough to be bothered with teaching them? I pray this is not so and ask you to join me in this petition that all of us might kindle a greater love for those we need to reach with the gospel.

W stands for WISDOM. "And they that are wise shall shine as the brightness of the firmament; and they that turn many to righteousness as the stars forever and ever (Daniel 12:3). "The fruit of the righteous is a tree of life; and he that is wise winneth souls" (Proverbs 11:30).

What a shock to some of our more "intellectual" Christian brethren! A mark of true wisdom is involvement in personal evangelism! This is exactly what God teaches and man must heed it. The only wisdom which will have eternal value is that applied to the work of God. For the fruit we bear will be the basis of our eternal reward. Winning a soul to Christ is one of the best possible examples of fruit in the productive life of the Christian.

O stands for OPPORTUNITIES. Matthew 25:14-30 relates the parable of the talents (opportunities). The most valuable lesson we can learn from this is that each person has at least one; no one is empty-handed. A lot of us give the excuse of not having the opportunity to teach others. In reality we have simply blinded ourselves to those at hand. I believe that each of us are surrounded with a multiplicity of occasions to tell another of Christ. Our prayer should be for wisdom to see these and the courage to accept them!

R stands for REASON. "To you that are afflicted rest with us, at the revelation of the Lord Jesus, from heaven with the angels of his power in flaming fire, rendering vengeance to them that know not God, and to them that obey not the gospel of our Lord Jesus, who shall suffer punishment, even eternal destruction from the face of the Lord and from the glory of his might" (II Thessalonians 1:7-9).

What better reason could we have in teaching another than to save his soul from the unspeakably dreadful punishment waiting for those who do not obey? How can we possibly keep the Truth to ourselves with this certain knowledge of destruction for all the disobedient? Oh, awake, Christians, awake to the reason you became a child of God. Teach some one today! Or at least make a start!

K stands for KNOWLEDGE. "Study to show thyself approved unto God, a workman that needeth not to be ashamed, rightly dividing the word of truth" (II Timothy 2:15).

Here again we find the answer to the time-worn excuse "I don't know enough." The remedy is simple. Study. Yes, this takes time and effort, but everything worthwhile does. And read the first part of that scripture again! "To show thyself approved unto God." This is one method of proving our acceptability to our Creator—study. How careless we are when it comes to our spiritual education. We expend great amounts of time and untold energy to educate ourselves in worldly knowledge. But our spiritual learning is still often on the kindergarten level! You can't teach that which you do not know, but if you knew enough to become a Christian yourself, you have the start of enough knowledge to teach others. Now, build on that foundation!

We have taken the internal letters of personal work and gained a little more insight into this area of service. I daresay that some of you will still say "I can't teach others." And if I could read your innermost thoughts, I believe I would find one word inscribed there—FEAR! Be honest, admit that fear and begin to overcome it. Besides, you have probably just shut yourself off from the source that will erase any misgivings you have. Let me close this lesson on a positive note. Read and accept II Timothy 1:7. "For God gave us not a spirit of fearfulness; but of power and love and discipline." Don't be afraid but find that first person to tell of God's way! He may be standing right beside you.
Further exercise in PERSONAL WORK :

P also stands for purpose, preparation, pleasant, perseverance, power, perfection, participation, partner and patience!
E also stands for enthusiasm, earnest, eager, encourage and energy!
R also stands for realistic, redemption, rejoicing, remedy and restraint!
S also stands for serenity, stability, steadfast, skill, service, satisfaction, security and success!

O also stands for obedience, orderly, opinion, and obligation!

N also stands for naturalness, nobility, newness, nourishment and nurture!

A also stands for ability, achievement, action, ambition, answer and appeal!

L also stands for labor, learner, life and listen!

W also stands for warning, wonderful, workman, win, willingness and wholesome!

O also stands for organization, ornament, original and outstanding!

R also stands for ready, reflect, regular, respect and reputation!

K also stands for keeper, kind, kingdom, kindred and kneel!

TO THINK UPON

1. See how many other characteristics or qualities or attitudes involved in personal work you can find starting with the letters of the words.

2. What do you feel is your greatest hindrance in doing personal work? Why?

3. What is the danger in feeling that evangelism is the work of the minister alone?

4. Do you have a program of personal work going in your congregation? If not, why not discuss it with your elders or the minister and see if you cannot get some plan going.

5. Make a survey of how many baptisms were accomplished in the past year in your local group and how many additions came from Christians placing membership. Which is greater? What can you do to enlarge the first number?

CHAPTER X

"AUDIENCE PARTICIPATION"

What would a Christian from the first century think if he were able to attend the worship services of our congregation this Sunday? Do you think he could readily perceive that he had not stumbled into the wrong place? How would the mechanics of our worship compare with what he was used to? Would he feel as close to God after this attendance or do you think he might come away scratching his head, puzzling over what kind of social ritual he had just witnessed? I cannot help but feel that if his worship granted satisfaction to him, it would be because he had been schooled in the proper personal attitude toward such service and not from any great spiritual atmosphere on our part.

This is not meant to be a condemnation or criticism of the worship of the church. It is intended as a warning against a way toward which too many groups are drifting and as an admonition for the individual Christian to awaken to his responsibility in the worship. Too long we have been a part of the audience, expecting to be "entertained" and uplifted on Sunday morning and evening. Too long we have felt the song leader and the preacher were responsible for making the worship spiritually acceptable. They have an important place, but by far the most essential part is played by each individual Christian seeking to find his God and worship Him and to give that God the opportunity to reach the human soul.

When I say that the church has become preacher oriented, I am not casting disparagement upon those worthy men who have devoted their lives to serving God. The chiding does not belong to them but rather to the thousands of members of the church who are satisfied to let their worship become a matter of a good sermon on Sunday. Now be honest, how many of us judge the value of our worship by how the preacher's words struck us that morning? This very attitude has served to take the spirituality from Christian worship and place the emphasis on a ritualistic observance of two songs, a prayer, another song, communion, another song and then a sermon. Then we leave the building feeling somehow cheated but never really understanding why.

I wonder how many thousands of people are passing up the richest opportunity of their lives each Sunday? I am not talking about those who miss worship every Lord's Day. I am speaking of those who are in attendance, and I might add, very faithful attendance. Yet they have never learned how to use the limitless power available to them during this period of worship. They came so close to the "current" but never once have they made the effort to "plug in" and reap the spiritual benefits of true communion with their God. They are mere spectators at a feast so rich and wondrous as to nourish their soul to face the day ahead. So near and yet how many come away spiritually starved! It is no wonder that such religion does not carry over into the weekday world! it barely sustains one through that first day.

WORSHIP MEANS DIFFERENT THINGS TO DIFFERENT PEOPLE. To some, coming to worship gives them the opportunity to see friends and enjoy some kind of social fellowship. Others look at worship as the ritual which they perform in order to be a member of the church. Their church membership is more important than the worship instead of both being an integrated part of their religious service. But to a large percentage of Christians worship is a duty which they know must be performed and by which, in some way they don't quite understand, **God is given His due!** When the twelve o'clock whistle blows on Sunday, their religious experience is over for the week and these spectators go home to relax.

There are those, however, who have come to know what true worship is and by becoming personally involved in it, have strengthened their life with every hour of participation. Those are the ones who have learned that to worship in Truth is not enough and have let their spirit be included in this precious period when God and His Spirit and man and his spirit seek and find each attuned to the other!

Acceptable worship can include the use of a song leader and also a minister to proclaim the word. But when we tend to look upon these as "professionals" and us as "audience," we separate the church into the categories of clergy and laity just as surely as does the denominational world. Christians are quick to state that in the church of Christ there is no such distinction, but by our very actions we prove otherwise. Elton Trueblood states that "too many are merely back-seat Christians, willing to be observers of a performance which the professionals put on, ready to criticize or to applaud, but not willing even to consider the possibility of real participation. While thousands claim to have some sort of connection with a church, it is not a connection of **involvement.** The result is bound to be superficiality. Whatever the nature of the situation, only the involved ever really know anything thoroughly."

The church does not need these "back-seat" Christians; it does need, however, the personal involvement of each of its members. What wonders of weekday Christianity we would witness, if more of us would stop being mere spectators and start participating in the power of true worship and the vital, enriching experience it provides.

PURPOSE OF WORSHIP IS TWOFOLD. First, and most important, it honors and magnifies God. As human beings we approach God and bow in adoration, wonder and praise. This is the blessed privilege our Father has granted in allowing us to worship Him. In prostrating ourselves spiritually before God in our worship, we find the second purpose of this service. At the same time we exalt our Maker, we are strengthening and edifying our own weak nature! How wonderful that God has ordained that the act of honoring Him should also greatly benefit the one involved in the worship!

We must be careful, however, lest our worship become exclusively that of calling God to come to us. It must not be one-sided. Our first duty in this privilege is to bring ourselves before Him, in humility recognizing our unworthy position and yet in gratitude that we may approach this near to bring our praise and adoration. Then we have no need to worry about His part; it is assured. When we bow before Him in worship, His Spirit blends with ours to furnish us the edification we so need to face the problems of the world.

Knowing how to worship is not an inborn trait nor is it a gift at the time of our conversion. It is an acquired practice and comes from self-discipline, knowledge and training. Stafford North has written an excellent tract pointing this out quite clearly. It is called "Learning the Fine Art of Worship." It is so well-written that I would encourage every Christian to obtain a copy and make it a part of their study material. Brother North emphasizes three requirements in learning how to worship and I am going to include them in our lesson.

WORSHIP REQUIRES LIVING CLOSE TO GOD. This seems most elementary yet how vital it is to be close to and love that which we are going to worship. Something in man's nature seems to demand worship but unenlightened people usually choose that which they do not know and thus fear, as the basis for their worship. God has allowed that we know Him by revelation through the word and through His Son's coming to this earth. He did not leave it up to our intuition or instinct to find Him. Of course, we will never fully know God until we are face to face in eternity. But He has revealed enough to allow us to understand who we worship.

It is ridiculous to assume that a person can worship acceptably a God they know only through a ritual of services on Sunday. Christianity is not a one-day-a-week religion but is a full-time purpose of life. Only when we live with God daily and know Him intimately in every area of our life, can we begin to feel the desire to exalt and honor Him. Only in total commitment of our life to His care and service can we truly reach the heights of worship which will be a sweet savor to God and a blessing of strength to us.

God loved us; He sent His Son to die for our sins! Only when we grasp the meaning of this in our own life, can we express genuine praise and gratitude to our Father who has redeemed us from destruction through the death of Jesus. A deep understanding of this love will make worship meaningful to us. No one will have to **command** us to worship God any more than "someone has to command you to appreciate a beautiful sunset." It is simply magnificent and so majestic that you cannot help but stand in awe and wonder. Just so our worship of God if we see the glory and majesty of what He is in our life.

WORSHIP REQUIRES CAREFUL PREPARATION. We accept the necessity to prepare for any worthwhile endeavor of life. We prepare for our careers, for marriage, for social occasions and for teaching a lesson. We make elaborate preparations for special meals and to prepare food for freezing or canning, looking to the future. We should realize the importance of the fact that when we go to the church building on Sunday for worship, we are literally entering the presence of God. True, He is not visible but He is there as surely as the minister, the song leader, the teachers and all those in the audience. Dare we come into His presence without preparation of any kind? How presumptuous we human beings are!

Brother North says that the first step in preparing for worship is to understand the acts of worship which God has specified. We know that Christian worship in Truth is witnessed in five ways—the Lord's Supper, praying, singing, preaching and giving. The understanding of these areas of our worship is where the "spirit" part comes in. Christ said in John 4:23, 24 that true worshipers would be those who worship in spirit and truth. We must not only include the necessary items but we must know why we use them and possess the correct attitude of heart in participating in them. A study of each of these will be given later in this lesson.

After a proper understanding of the acts which we perform in worship, I feel the most vital area of preparation comes in training the mind to be ready for coming into the presence of God. While the first step mentioned above is more or less a matter of one-time preparation, this second step is one that must be done each Lord's Day. It cannot be done one time and then expect it to be an automatic thing each week. The act would then become ritualistic and less important. Fresh thought control is desirable to center the heart on just what it will be doing on this special day of the week.

ARISE IN PLENTY OF TIME EACH SUNDAY. A usual picture of a Christian household on Sunday morning goes something like this: everyone sleeps later than they should because they were up too late on Saturday night. The mother rushes to get breakfast on the table, pushing the family to finish the meal. Frantically she tries to find enough clothing to go around and sometimes she will have to iron a shirt or dress. Finally the family is rushed to the car and father hurriedly drives to the building. They go to class out of breath and usually, out-of-sorts.

The mother should see that the family is up in plenty of time to eat properly and dress leisurely. She has prepared ahead of time in order that all the family has clean clothes, fresh and ready to put on. She is able to "be calm in her soul" and to allow her family to be the same. They arrive at Bible school ready to hear the word of God and later, ready to go into worship services because someone cared enough to prepare ahead of time.

Worship is a state of mind, coupled with certain bodily actions. Therefore it is necessary to make certain that the mind is as free from worldly cares, strife or any other disconcerting thought before we go before God in worship. The hour spent in Bible class helps do this to a great extent but somehow it fails to completely succeed. For what kind of scene do we have after the bell rings signaling the close of Bible study? Children noisily scurrying to and fro; adults loudly visiting with one another and passing into the main auditorium of the building. Noise and confusion usually reign!

When we bring visitors to our services, we always find the occasion to ask what their feelings were. We have been shocked at their answers. Without exception they have all said something to this effect, "Your congregation has very little reverence!" We were ashamed but we had to admit they were right. Of course, we know that often their conception of a church is the physical building and they look upon these facilities as a holy place. We recognize that the building is not the church; nor is it holy. **BUT THE REASON WE COME TO THAT BUILDING IS HOLY!** And our attitudes and actions should prove that to those around us.

One congregation felt the need to combat this general lackadaisical attitude of coming into worship. They had each teacher remind their pupils at the close of the class period that they were about to pass into the presence of the Creator for the purpose of worshiping Him. They asked each one to be careful of their actions and words because they would not want to appear disrespectful to God. From this came a new awareness of the purpose of worship and great good was accomplished for the members as well as the visitors who came their way.

WORSHIP REQUIRES INDIVIDUAL PARTICIPATION. In doing everything "decently and in order" we have set a pattern for our worship which calls for the individual to sit quietly through most of the service. The preacher, song director and others take the lead. This has brought on the "spectator-performer" situation which we spoke of previously. Again this is no criticism of this method of worship, but rather a warning lest it become so entrenched as tradition in our minds so that we feel we are not an active part of worship.

Elton Trueblood in his **Company of the Committed** gives an interesting picture concerning the possible method of worship in the early church. "An indication of procedure is provided by Colossians 3:16 when we read 'as you teach and admonish one another in all wisdom.' These words suggest a group of Christians sitting in some simple room, sharing with one another their hopes, their failures, and their prayers. The key words are **one another.** There are no mere observors or auditors; all are involved. Each is in the ministry; each needs the advice of the others; and each has something to say to the others. This picture of mutual admonition seems strange to modern man, but perhaps that strangeness is a measure of our decline from something of amazing power."

He further stated that this mutual participation was what prompted Paul to warn them not to talk all at once, but one at a time (I Corinthians 14:31). In a gathering of this sort, it would be best that women sit quietly and not take the authority from the men by a prominent part in the worship. Thus it was that Paul told them not to allow women to speak in the churches (I Corinthians 14:34, 35). We take this to mean we are not to have women preachers (and rightly so) but this command would be so much more logical to understand if we pictured the early church worship in such a setting.

I am not urging a return to this way of worship. In our larger congregations it would be almost impossible to achieve in an orderly fashion. Yet I do feel that our worship has become more impersonal because of the very necessity of the order of worship we use exclusively today. There is less challenge to be actually **involved** in the worship and because this is true, there is an even greater responsibility on us to make certain we are not just spectators in this communion with God.

Let us now look at each item of worship and see how we can participate as an individual.

THE LORD'S SUPPER. Scriptures: I Corinthians 10:16, 17. I Corinthians 11:23-29. This memorial feast was instituted by Christ before His death and delivered unto the Apostles. They were then commanded to teach all the things which Christ had given them. It was the practice of the early church to eat of this supper on the first day of the week. Paul himself received it as a teaching directly from Christ and followed His instructions by teaching it faithfully to others.

To partake of the Lord's Supper in Truth, we must use the proper elements (unleavened bread and fruit of the vine) at the proper time (each Lord's Day). To partake of it in the spirit (which is usually the heart of individual participation) our heart and mind must be centered on Christ, His death and His resurrection. All worldly thoughts must be thrust from us as we commune with God in memory of what His love gave man. I Corinthians 11:27-29 gives further instructions as to the danger of not being **involved** in this communion. The manner in which we eat of this memorial is of vital importance for by an absent-minded or irreverent participation, we can actually be damning our soul.

Individual involvement in the Lord's Supper carries with it a complete submitting of our mind to the Savior who loved us so much He made His perfect sacrifice so that we might have redemption of our sins. Our love for God and Christ wells up in our hearts as we partake of the bread and fruit of the vine and with this surging upward, their Spirit becomes one with ours and we are renewed inwardly.

PRAYING. In our public worship, the prayers that are offered are done so by one person at a time voicing a petition for the whole group. This is a necessity because bedlam would result if each tried to offer a vocal entreaty to God. However, this does not excuse the personal participation in this element of worship. Our thoughts must be focused on the words of the one praying and at the same time silent words go upward from us. Times of general public prayer are meaningful indeed for this is a literal prostration of our spiritual beings before the throne of grace. If our mind is straying to other thoughts or we become distracted, it is the same as if we were to stand up spiritually and walk away from the throne! Thoughtful concentration is d i f f i c u l t and yet with love motivating us, it becomes easier with practice.

SINGING. This is one area of worship where even the audience participates outwardly. Yet it is also a much neglected phase because the songs have become so familiar to us that we can mouth the words without having the meaning touch our heart. Or we become interested in the clothing of others or their actions or our thoughts stray so that we forget the very purpose of the music. I feel that God commanded vocal music from His children because it involved personal participation whereas with instrumental music, another could offer the worship and the majority would be left untouched.

One purpose of singing other than worship to God is to admonish and exhort fellow Christians. Sometimes we put so much emphasis on the song director or on the correct tone and key that we are not worshiping nor exhorting but something more akin to entertaining ourselves and others. Certainly we should strive to make our singing as sweet and correct as possible, but in the end, the sound is not that which is so important. God is not listening to the music for the sheer beauty of the strains of the song; He is tuned to the melody coming from the heart. While it is pleasant for the human ear to hear lovely music, it is more needful that we heed the words and their depth of meaning. Whatever the kind of song we are singing—psalms, hymns or spiritual songs—our heart must be aware of the words and then our lips can issue the notes carrying their message to God and to our fellow Christians.

GIVING. This, too, is an area of worship where each individual can participate outwardly. But the great danger here is not the failure to participate but rather the motive behind that participation. First, as stewards of the blessings granted us by God (and everything we have comes from Him) we will have to give an accounting of how we used all these gifts. If the heart is given in love and the whole of life as a sacrifice to Him, then we could be assured our financial giving would be acceptable. Personal involvement in returning a portion unto God should be done only after a serious purposing—evaluating not "how little can I give" but "how little can I keep for myself." This purposing serves as a basis which we can use in setting up a budget for our income and it can also be of value to the planning of the church's program. If the elders know how much the congregation will give (unless providentially hindered), they can set up a more active and realistic outline of work.

Our attitude must be one of cheerfulness, exhibiting the gratitude that we can do something in return for all the bounteous gifts He has bestowed upon us. If this is how we feel, our offering will not be grudging but given freely. And best of all, this is a wondrous way to lay up treasure in heaven. Any earthly investment we might make will not pay nearly so large a dividend in the end. Personal participation brings the greater amount of personal satisfaction and reward.

PREACHING. Audience participation in this area of worship comes from learning how to listen with both the ears and the heart. The physical organs of hearing need little training to hear the words spoken by the preacher but it is a little more difficult to keep the mind tuned in. Each of us should clear our thoughts of any disturbing elements and focus our attention on the words which will help us in living the daily life. I often wonder what the minister thinks as he looks out across the audience and sees the blank stares of some; the nodding heads of others and the complete inattentiveness of still others. If this servant of God has taken the time to prepare a lesson from the Bible, we should spend at least some time in preparing our minds to be receptive ground for the seed he can plant. Audience participation in the sermon is like the "vitamins" we can take to keep our spiritual life healthy and fruitful. These words of edification and exhortation are not for the purpose of entertainment but to help us lead the acceptable life in the service of God.

CUT AND DRIED? Norvel Young recently wrote an article entitled "Cut and Dried." In it he gives some suggestions that he feels might keep our worship services from being routine, ritualistic and "cut and dried."

1. "Let more time be spent in prayerfully planning each hour of worship. Frequently the same schedule is followed year after year because no one thinks about how it can be improved. The Bible does not prescribe a set ritual outlining the order of songs, prayers and sermons. God left this arrangement to our judgment. Let us not neglect to plan carefully and not set a tradition which prevails because no one takes time to change it."

2. "Vary the time devoted to different parts of worship. Variety will help prevent boredom on the part of the less mature Christian. Some congregations never change the order of the Sunday morning worship. You can almost set your watch by the time the preacher begins his sermon. And the same number of songs are sung at the same time and the same number of prayers are prayed at the same point and time."

"No wonder our children think this is "cut and dried." Young people realize that this procedure year after year indicates a lack of thought about how the worship can be most effective and pleasing to God. Scriptural worship is to be in spirit and truth. Surely there are times when we could profitably spend thirty or forty minutes worshiping around the Lord's table. Perhaps more Bible reading and more songs could be used to focus attention on the remembrance of the Lord's sacrifice. Or, again, more stress could be placed on our "laying by in store."

One of the most valuable ways to make our worship more spiritual was introduced to our congregation this summer by a young Christian just completing his first year at York College. He went to great effort and spent much time to see that all the songs were coordinated with the thought of the day's sermon. The routine of the worship was changed each Sunday to give more variety. There was more Bible reading and it, too, was related to the message given. He even spoke to those leading the prayers and asked that they make special mention of the particular subject which was to be brought by the minister. Yes, there was discontent and grumbling on the part of some; others even said it wasn't scriptural! But it has done more to help me and others worship in spirit than the thoughtless routine of the previous years.

God created us in His own image. Since we know this is not our physical body, we recognize that we are spiritual beings in His image. The very purpose of our existence here on earth is to serve and worship our Creator (Ecclesiates 12:13 and Matthew 4:10). We have the need for spiritual food and communion with God in order that our inner being be nourished and strengthened. Recharging our batteries, so to speak, for the long pull in the week ahead. This is another reason why God commands us to gather together in spiritual fellowship with other Christians and exhorts us not "to forsake the assembling of ourselves together."

Failure to worship God is a symptom of the real disease. That disease is a lack of faith in God's commandments and promises and a lack of love for God and for spiritual things. If we do not love God enough to come to worship, why would we want to spend eternity with Him?

At the very heart of worship, of course, is the necessity for attendance at the services set aside by the command of God for this purpose. Would I absent myself if I knew Christ and His Father were going to be sitting in a front pew next Sunday? Certainly not! But they are there every Sunday—not sitting in that pew—but with every Christian. Dare I take myself from the divine presence for selfish and foolish reasons?

There's a story told about a Chinese gentleman who was traveling through the country. He owned seven coins he carried on a string. Beside the road he saw a poor beggar and compassionately gave him six of the coins. The beggar went away and the gentleman found a place to spend the night. As he slept, the beggar slipped up and stole the seventh coin. With horror we immediately accuse the beggar of unrighteousness. But we should be careful lest we condemn ourselves. God has given us six days out of the compassion of His heart to let us use for our work and pleasure. One day He has designated as a time for worship. How many of us are not content with the six days but steal and pervert the seventh to our way?

Russia is atheistic. Sundays are spent hiking in the mountains, boat riding, or strolling in the park. Yet Sundays mean about the same thing to the "average" American. However Russia is at least consistent for she believes there is no God. We boast of being a "Christian" nation, yet our actions prove the opposite. The Chief Justice of our Supreme Court said, "People of all religions and people with no religion are beginning to regard Sunday as a time for family activity, for late sleeping, for passive and active entertainments, for dining and the like. Such activities may not be harmful within themselves but they must not crowd God out of our lives if we are to please Him. No wonder our Russian visitors think we are hypocrites!"

Sad, too, is the fact that many Christians may be found among those perverting the Lord's Day from a time of worship to a time for their own willful desires. Can we not accept the fact that worship is not a distasteful duty which must be performed, but rather a joyful giving of self in praise and honor to God. Who, in return, will provide the blessed comfort and strength we so desperately need to live the other days. David was a master of worshipful praise in his psalms. I urge you to read some of them every day until your spirit is more able to voice your own feelings of exaltation toward God. "Exalt ye the Lord, and worship at his footstool; for he is holy" (Psalm 22:5). Search out these beautiful psalms of worship and honor unto Jehovah. They will enrich your life beyond measure.

Worship is a personal experience with God. If I come away from the Sunday services with unfilled longings and no sense of having communed with God, I have not truly worshiped. I can blame no one for others cannot worship for me. It is a person-to-person relationship with Christ and the Father. A time for upward reachings and for spiritual renewment. Until I participate as a person, the Sunday worship will be no more than a formal display of my religious leanings evidenced by mere attendance. Deep personal worship will show itself in an attitude like David's when he said, "I was glad when they said unto me, Let us go into the house of the Lord" (Psalm 122:1). Can I say this about my worship?

TO THINK UPON

1. Discuss how ritualistic our worship might become and how we can avoid this.

2. Why is personal participation so necessary in worship?

3. How can we better train our children to worship acceptably?

4. Discuss ways to make the time between classes and worship move more quietly and smoothly. Discuss what effect our confusion has upon visitors.

5. Is it possible to worship in Truth and not in spirit? Do you feel it is possible to worship in spirit and not in Truth?

CHAPTER XI

"THE MOST UNEXPLORED FRONTIER IN THE WORLD"

With the passage of time and aided by the adventure-seeking nature of man, there are few frontiers left on this planet earth to explore. This is revealed so vividly in the present efforts of nations to reach out to the frontiers beyond the barrier of space. Man, for some deep intuitive reason, cannot let the unknown remain outside his experience and knowledge without making some great endeavor to explore and claim its benefits as his own. This fever of inquiry into the undefined has brought civilization much good. We now have more land area in which to live and produce food and raw materials for use in the ever-growing processes of product manufacture. Our health is more securely protected by the vast advances made in the medical world. New techniques are being uncovered every day and man seems ever restless to find new "worlds to conquer."

So much of this spirit of exploration, however, is limited to the physical world alone. Only a select group of scholars ever spend much time in seeking out new frontiers of spirituality which could possibly be of more help than any material discovery or invention. I am not speaking, of course, of the new man-made theories and philosophies which have been prevalent since man first started using his ability to think for himself. Rather I am speaking of the areas of spiritual life which still remain largely untouched or unexplored by the lives of human beings. These are the principles given us by God, but for unknown reasons, have not been fathomed to seek true understanding nor accepted completely into our way of life. In viewing the history of mankind, both secular and divine, I am moved to say that perhaps the most unexplored frontier of this sort lies near us and all around but we seem to ignore it most of the time. This frontier is that of **love.**

How can I say that this is an unexplored frontier when man has always been interested in it? He even accepts some of it for his good. Yes, these things are true, but in reality, mankind has only taken a part of it and built of that his own product, limiting its usefulness and power by failing to recognize its source and its true meaning. Perhaps some have caught this vision of divine power and have made it a living part of their life. These are the fortunate ones, but they are so few compared to the human race as a whole. Free your mind from the shackles of earth-ties and let it soar toward the infinite. Can you even imagine what this world would be like if even one-third of its inhabitants had fully explored Love and made its values theirs? What changes would be wrought! What peace and genuine fellowship would prevail! Now look at the ugliness of man's attitude toward and his relationship with other men. Man's inhumanity to man! Can you not see why I say that Love is the most unexplored frontier in all the world?

Bring this even closer to home. What governs the association of Christian with fellow Christian? Have we in the church really had much more success in penetrating the borders of Love? Do we not have to admit that most of the problems in our congregation are not caused by spiritual weakness, financial difficulties or lack of zeal? We may be plagued with these but if we are honest, we will concede that a drouth of Love is actually at the root of all problems we have. The ones listed above are mere symptoms of what really ails us. Therefore the great need in the Christian life today is for more understanding of what Love is and more acceptance of its influence in our activities.

Psychiatrist William C. Menninger, in a talk in Oklahoma City, commented, "Individual capacity to love is the hope of the world." We agree with this great medical man but this statement can have little meaning unless we understand just what Love is. Only then can we place its importance at the correct value and truly utilize its power for good in the world.

The most basic definition of Love is found in I John 4:8. There we are told "God is love." This is its fullest and most complete meaning. Yet because our finite mind cannot grasp the infinite depth of all that this implies, we still must search further. And perhaps we should not look for a definition as much as seek out the qualities of Love and how it acts. This we can understand and in this knowledge, take it into our life and live it in daily practice.

Because the human mind cannot fully know God nor what He is, we do not perceive the expression "God is love." But show us the things that God does and the manner in which He acts toward others and it becomes clear. "Herein was the love of God manifested in us, that God hath sent his only begotten Son into the world that we might live through him. Herein is love, not that we loved God, but that he loved us, and sent his Son to be the propitiation for our sins. Beloved, if God so loved us, we also ought to love one another. No man hath beheld God at any time: if we love one another, God abideth in us, and his love is perfected in us" (I John 4:9-12).

Go to your Bible and seek out all the passages which refer to God's love. They all have one thing in common—"God loved, so He gave" or "God loved, so He did." This would give us the first clue as to the true meaning of Love. Its foremost characteristic is an active quality which evidences itself in giving to others, in pouring out its feelings in deeds of kindness and warmth.

TRUE LOVE IS UNSELFISH. God's love is the prime example of this and so is Christ's. Each loved man and each thought of what was best for these earthly creatures. No thought of self kept them from giving and doing that which could bring the greatest blessings for the ones they loved. Even though we are human, we can practice this same quality and in so doing, bring a power of divinity into our life. If God is love, then surely that love, when it is utilized as a procedure of human life, will link us to the power of its source.

Our love must not be passive but an active moving potency, seeking out and performing that which is good for the ones we love. Kahlil Gibran in his **The Prophet** pictures this force in practice when he says, "Work is love made visible." And only when it becomes visible will it affect the lives of mankind.

TRUE LOVE IS RECIPROCAL. In other words, the more you give, the more you get. The poet Edwin Markham states it this way, "There is a destiny which makes us brothers; none goes his way alone. All that is sent into the lives of others, comes back into our own." Another person described it this way, "The love that makes us brothers has the magic qualities of radar. It hits the mark, then, enriched, wings its way back to the sender." Could this be what God had in mind in all His acts of love? That man should feel the touch of its beauty and send it back to his Creator enriched by his own love. Surely our God must appreciate a love returned so freely, with praise and thanksgiving. Even in His divinity, our weak yearnings must seem precious. If His love has touched us, then let us send our own winging in return to the majesty of His throne—and to our fellow man.

Our children sometimes say they love us "a whole bushel." Perhaps this idea of love being a certain supply keeps us from giving more away. Can we feel that if we give out so many "bushels" we will have none left? True love is not a matter of supply; it is unlimited. Dr. Frank Crane's essay says it this way, "Give it away, throw it away, splash it over, empty your pockets, shake the basket, turn the glass upside down, and tomorrow you shall have more than ever." For love is not a supply, but an ability. Cultivate the ability and it is unlimited. Once a person has learned to compose beautiful music, he need not worry about his supply of notes— only how to use them in glorious combinations. Just so, the ability to love!

TRUE LOVE IS GOOD MEDICINE. The need for love is the most universal of human characteristics. We need it from the moment we draw our first breath. Deprive a person of love and soon even the physical being will become affected. One of the most effective ways of medical treatment for those who are ill—physically or mentally—is to give them a reassurance that some one does care for them. This is especially good in the area of mental illness. At the Menninger Clinic in Kansas love is actually prescribed on the patients' charts when their needs are so evident. These same charts later record the almost miraculous recovery when liberal doses of the "medicine" were applied. To be loved is to feel secure and security of life and spirit does more to keep a person healthy than any other thing.

WHAT TRUE LOVE IS NOT. Love has been called the greatest word in the English language. Howard Whitman said, "Undoubtedly more people have lived for it than have lived for money, fame or pleasure. And probably more people have died for it, or lack of it, than have died from cancer or bad hearts." It may be the greatest word, but it is also the most misunderstood. Modern man has taken this one word and endowed it with a multiplicity of meanings. We say we "love" everything from apple pie to our family. We use the same word but do we mean the same thing? From a perusal of today's movies, magazines and books, one might think that love is purely a physical attraction of the male for the female and vice versa. While sex is certainly a part of true married love, it is not true love within itself. The Greeks did not have this same difficulty with their language for they had many words to express the different feelings possessed toward objects and people. But we are stuck with just the one word **love** and we must be careful of its use lest we degrade its real meaning and its value be lost to future generations. When we wish to denote certain emotions toward things, let us learn to increase our vocabulary so that we can choose other words that will adequately describe how we feel. Should we not reserve **love** for the truer, deeper sentiments of the heart?

These can be distinguished from the baser, more trivial feelings by certain characteristics which reveal genuine love. We will list five of these identifying qualities of real love.

1. INTEREST. If we really love a person, we will have a sincere interest in him. We will be concerned with his problems, his thoughts, his needs, what he stands for, and what makes him happy. Our actions toward that one will be motivated by how we can best fill the areas of interest we have in his life. We will appreciate that one as a human being and do everything in our power to bring him to his fullest potential of life.

2. CARE. The Italians have a lovely way of expressing love. It is "Ti voglio bene," which literally means "I desire your well-being." This beautiful way of voicing this deep emotion shows the true direction of love. If I care for another, I will desire that one's welfare. But my desire will not stop there for love is active. I will go on to **do** something to promote the well-being of my loved one. I will care what happens to him

and will judge my actions to best protect him or to bring about good in his life.

3. PRODUCTIVITY. At the same time, I will make certain that my acts for his welfare do not deny him his own independence. What I do will help him grow and develop into a worthwhile person. I will not "smother" my loved one and rob him of being busy and productive in his own right. True love will inspire the loved one to use his talents and resources to the full. Both the lover and the loved one must be creative, productive people. True love does not cripple another in the name of his own welfare.

4. RESPONSIBILITY. "Am I my brother's keeper?" is not the attitude of true love. Nor does it urge that "George do it." My love for another will be willing to accept a tender sense of responsibility toward him. It will not overwhelm nor dominate but support, guide and assist. Love makes every man his brother's keeper.

5. RESPECT. Nothing we own is more valuable than our personal integrity. When we love another, we respect his integrity. "Integrity is that wholeness, the complete package which makes each an individual in his own right." To love another means we will respect him for what he is even though that might not be our own preference. We may not approve of his actions, his beliefs nor his personality, but we will respect his right to be different if we love him. This does not mean we cannot help him become a better person but only that we do not try to mold him after our own opinions, desires and pattern of life.

If our feelings toward another can measure up to these standards, we may be assured we are beginning to understand a little of the power of the love God intends for man to possess. These five checkpoints should be used no matter what the basic relationship between the two people. Since our life is made up of so many of these relationships, love should be the "lubrication" which allows them to run smoothly. Let's turn our attention to some of these different areas of life.

MAN'S LOVE FOR GOD. This love shows itself by living as close as possible to our Creator. In fact, a proof of our love is whether we keep His commandments (I John 5:3). Another active example of our love for God is shown in the worship we present to Him. This was discussed in a previous chapter and you might want to bring up some of the qualities which make this worship more meaningful to us and pleasing unto God.

Gibran, the poet wrote, "When you love you should not say 'God is in my heart,' but rather 'I am in the heart of God.'" Gibran's biographer commented on these lines saying, "How can one who is in the heart of God feel any barriers between himself and God or even another man? Would he not feel all men dwelling in himself and himself dwelling in every man? Can one so unified with all creation ever say, I have given so much to my neighbor or have taken so much from my neighbor? Does he not become a taker when giving, and a giver when taking?" To love God is to be a part of Him and living in Him and He in us until our will and purposes are one. This will flow from our heart and life into the lives of our fellow man; for if we love God, we must love our fellow man.

MAN'S LOVE FOR FELLOW MAN. I John 4:21 makes the bold statement that the one who loves God will also love other human beings! Yet how literally do we take this? Not very, I'm afraid, because daily we see the conflicts of hate and strife issuing from one to another. The Christian's attitude must of necessity go back to what John wrote. If we hate others, we cannot love God. The secret, then, must lie in becoming closer to God and letting His will and way become ours. Since it is within the nature of God to love all, even those who are unloveable, we can approach this standard by becoming more at one with Him. Then His nature can blend with ours and together we can love our fellow man.

LOVE MUST ALSO ENCOMPASS OUR ENEMY. We are often puzzled why God would ask such a thing of us. How can we love those who mistreat us and hate us, as much as we love those near and dear to us? "Impossible" we say. A close study of the original words used in this command will help us better comprehend this attitude we must have toward our enemy. This is a good illustration of the advantage the Greek language had in defining the degrees of love. They had several words which we have translated simply **love** but in the original had a different shade of meaning. The word used to describe our feeling toward God was different from that which signified a brotherly love, a married love or the one which describes our feelings toward the enemy. This latter did not involve the emotions since we would find it impossible to have the proper feeling toward our adversaries if we let our emotions guide us. Instead God caused a word to be used which involves the will of man, his control of self. Thus, to "love" our enemy means we must control our feelings toward him. We do not actively seek evil for him but only desire his good. Our thoughts concerning him are controlled and brought into the light of God's love for us. He cared for us while we were yet sinners. To be like Him, we must have this same basic attitude toward those who are against us.

LOVE OF MAN AND WIFE. This was the first human love which God gave man. It was based on mutual needs and their fulfillment. Adam needed a suitable companion and woman was created to fill that need. God did not have to tell Adam to love her for he immediately recognized this other person as a completion to himself. He said, "She is bone of my bone and flesh of my flesh." Eve possessed certain desires and needs and Adam was to fulfill those. Their bodies were united in God-sanctioned physical love and their spiritual beings were fused into mutual care and concern.

Woman was made subject to man because God knew this was best for us. Our sex has been fighting this almost from the beginning and it has caused us to place ourselves outside God's pattern. Our misery is our own fault, I admit, but I cannot help but think that if man would fully treat us as God commanded, then we would be more willing to accept our proper role. God said that man should love his wife as he does himself. Woman should submit herself to and respect her mate. If woman were truly loved as man's self, she would find it easier to serve and reverence him. I am not making excuses for us w h e n we remove ourselves from the right way. I am only trying to say that if each partner would fulfill his own duties as God gave them, both would find marriage a "paradise on earth." The divine scheme of life is best and to fight it — either man or woman — will only bring sorrow and trouble.

FAMILY LOVE. Just because there is a family unit of husband, wife and children does not insure that love will be present. But it does provide a "greenhouse" in which love can thrive — if it is nurtured. The family unit is the heart of all civilization. It is the launching pad which sends forth the individual into a sometimes hostile world. What kind of "missile" is sent forth is determined by the character of that family which molds and shapes it into either readiness or inadequacy to face life. Family love is more than instinct. We do not love our children simply because we protect them, snuggle them and provide for them. Even the animal does that for its young. That is only biology in action. Love goes beyond biology. As Howard Whitman says, "To what extent do we affirm our children as people? How much do we respect their integrity? Their individuality? To what extent do we help them grow independently — instead of dominating and possessing them?" These are the measures which allow us to rise above the animals.

Our love for family will meet the standards given at the start of this lesson — interest, care, productivity, responsibility, and respect. True love may have special emotions varying with the persons involved but the basic relationship can always be judged by these qualities. This is true whether the tie be husband-wife; parent-child; man-fellow man; or man-God.

In 1950 a conference on children and youth was held at the White House. It drafted a document known as the "Pledge to Children." Here are its six main points:

1. From your earliest infancy we will give you our love, so that you may grow with trust in yourself and in others.

2. We will recognize your worth as a person and we will help you to strengthen your sense of belonging.

3. We will help you to develop initiative and imagination, so that you may have the opportunity freely to create.

4. We will encourage your curiosity and your pride in workmanship, so that you may have the satisfaction that comes from achievement.

5. We will provide you with all opportunities possible to develop your faith in God.

6. We will respect your right to be yourself.

These were formulated by men yet their basic concept is found in the word of God. They will help any family if they are practiced. Yet we must not forget that family love must also have some negatives. For true love is as limiting as it is permissive. We forbid certain things as parents because we realize the harm which might come as a result of allowing the child to have its way. Love limits — but only for love's sake. Not to be cruel, dominating nor dogmatic. God has commanded that we love and care for our children and above all, "to bring them up in the nurture and admonition of the Lord." Family life places responsibility on the children also and God backs this up when He tells them to obey their parents "for this is right." Family love will allow each member to grow as a separate person but will knit the group together in love and mutual concern for each other.

LOVE OF SELF. A psychiatrist once said, "A person who does not like and approve of himself cannot be happy." This was the thought of the second chapter of this book. In it we stated that love for others must spring from a source of self-love (which in turn is rooted in love for God). This term is not very pleasant sounding to us for we are accustomed to think of loving self as a bad quality. We connect it with a conceited, self-centered person. The scripture which tells us to "love thy neighbor as ourself" was once paraphased by a rabbi to read "Thou shalt love thyself properly, and then thou wilt love thy neighbor." True love of self is not vanity nor egotism but simply a proper respect for the person you are.

Dr. Erich Fromm points out that "selfishness and self-love, far from being identical, are actually opposites. The selfish person does not love himself too much but too little; in fact he hates himself and he tries to cover up this failure to care for his real self by constant self-indulgence and praise." When we love ourself properly we have a quiet inner attitude of self-acceptance. We know we are not perfect but mere human beings and we do not hate ourselves for our failures by tormenting our lives with guilt feelings.

When asked for a brief prescription for good human relations, Howard Whitman said, "Treat all people as though they loved you." He explained that if you feel they love you, then you must feel lovable. If you feel lovable, then you love yourself. If you love yourself, then you reflect love toward others. If you reflect love toward others, then love, like a mirror image is reflected back at you.

LOVE OF COUNTRY. You may think it strange that I should include this love in our study yet it is of such importance to us that I could not leave it out. We know that all principalities and powers that be are allowed to rule as a direct favor of God (Romans 13:1). Perhaps one of the greatest blessings allowed Americans is this wonderful country of ours. God has granted this nation to be exalted far above any other and as a direct result every American enjoys material bounty beyond even the imagination of over half the present world. We even tend to feel that we deserve these things through some worth of our own. This is not so. Just because God has allowed us to bask in this sunlight of freedom does not mean it will always be ours. For no country is any stronger than its citizens.

Patriotism is almost a dead emotion today. Love of country has been replaced with a selfish concern for only the individual. Shall we allow our nation to be pulled down and trod under a pagan power simply because we didn't love it enough? Love for country measures up to the same five standards mentioned before. It is active, not desiring all for self, but seeking what is best for the majority.

Does this active love show itself in wild emotional behavior, trying to force others to feel as we do? I think not. True love for country is a quiet, stable thing. It is not just lip service, a mere repeating of a pledge of allegiance. It is a warm, persuasive feeling of belonging to an entity of purposeful, useful citizens. It takes pride in the flag for it remembers the lives which shed blood to allow it to wave freely today. It takes an interest in the politics of the nation, realizing that unless good men are elected, the government will be no better.

Mature love of America has nothing to do with how rich, or powerful, or well-equipped she is. Perhaps this is why other nations do not respect us because they realize you do not measure a country's value by such artificial means. They lose their admiration for us because we present a picture of strength based on material values rather than lasting, worthwhile ideals. We tend to love America only and shut out the rest of the world. True patriotism does not, for it is capable to love all that counts for good in the earth. Through my love for my immediate home, I can better love my nation. Through my love for my nation, I can love the world. Love begets love; it does not limit itself to a single unit.

An unknown poet felt that each citizen had a responsibility to serve his country and there was a way he could do it best. "Who serves his country best? Not he who guides her senates in debate, and makes the laws which are her prop and stay; not he who wears the poet's purple vest, and sings her songs of love and grief and fate. There is a better way. He serves his country best who lives pure life, and doeth righteous deed, and walks straight paths, however others stray. And leaves his sons as uttermost bequest, a stainless record which all may read: This is a better way." I put it in ever shorter form, "He serves his country best who is a true Christian."

Dean Roy Pearson of Newton Centre, Massachusetts, wrote an article entitled "Circle for Love" and I want to use it to close this chapter.

"So much of life is spent in keeping other people out of it. Private rooms and houses, private clubs and offices, private roads and beaches — with all of them the point is the same: This isn't your property. It's mine. Keep out! Of course, in one sense a circle that shuts out the world is needed by everyone. We all need places of refuge. We are all porcupines, and our quills are less troublesome if there is a little space around us.

"But there is another sense in which the bigness of a human being can be measured by the circles he draws to take the world in. Some of us are too small to draw a circle larger than ourselves. Others go a little further and include our families. Still others draw the line at the edges of their own race and color, their own social group or political party, their own religion or nation. And the people are too few who have the bigness of interest and compassion to draw a circle large enough for all.

"All of us go around in circles, and there are times when 'good fences make good neighbors.' But the smaller the circle, the smaller the man. A strong man is not afraid of people different from himself, and a wise man welcomes them. If he knows nothing else, he knows that human beings have no place to live except the earth and that unless we want to die together, we must learn to live together. But the wise man probably knows, too, that when he draws a circle to shut out his brother, he does less damage to his brother than he does to himself. He puts himself in solitary confinement, and he locks the door from the inside. He denies himself the riches of other men's experiences. He starves his own mind, and he hardens his own heart.

"When a wise man names his brothers, he draws no circle smaller than the first one ever drawn on the earth. In the beginning, God gave the world its shape. He made it **round!**"

> "He drew a circle that shut me out —
> Heretic, rebel, a thing to flout.
> But love and I had the will to win:
> We drew a circle that took him in."
> — Edwin Markham

TO THINK UPON

1. Why do you feel that love is so powerful?

2. Discuss some of the characteristics which we know about God that prove His love for us.

3. Why is respect so important in true love between any parties?

4. How can love serve as "medicine?"

5. Suggest that each member seek out someone in the congregation who especially needs love and make effort to provide that care and concern for them — a widow, lonely teenager, unmarried adult, etc.

CHAPTER XII

"My Heart — Christ's Home"

The most glorious promise given the Christian is the forgiveness of his sins and the hope of an eternal home with God. Almost as wonderful is the pledge given in John 14:23. "If a man love me, he will keep my word: and my Father will love him, and we will come unto him, and make our abode with him." This same promise is given in Ephesians 3:16 and in a modern translation reads, "That Christ may settle down and be at home in your hearts by faith." Surely we do not understand all that this entails but if it has become a reality in our lives, we do know the surety and comfort of it.

It is interesting to note that the same word is used in John 14:23 as when Jesus told them that he would go to "prepare a **place** for you . . . that where I am, ye may be also." Just as He was soon to go back to the Father to prepare a heavenly home for His followers, Christ assures them that they can provide a home for Him in their hearts. He desires this abode with His children and earnestly pleads that they allow Him to enter.

It is truly wonderful to think that our heart can be a home for our Savior. As I began to think along these lines, I naturally tried to correlate this with something I was familiar with and could better understand. I thought of a home and all that it represents and my heart was warmed to think that just such a relationship could be mine with my Lord. My mind compared a physical home with the heart and I began to wonder about the entry of Jesus into each part of such a spiritual home. Why not take this home on a room-to-room basis and allow Jesus to truly become "at home?" Thus, this lesson came into being.

We will use the physical rooms of a house to compare with the different areas of the human life. Of course, we understand the heart does not have separate rooms as such but the principles will be the same.

THE DOOR. This is the threshold to the home of the heart and like any door to a house, it has two positions — opened and closed. It is the sole decision of the owner of the heart as to whether the door opens to admit or remains closed to shut out. For there is a caller outside and he wishes entry. "Behold, I stand at the door and knock: if any man hear my voice and open the door, I will come in to him, and will sup with him, and he with me" (Revelation 3:20). Christ is waiting outside each heart and He pleads that we open the door and let Him in.

When I open the door to my heart and admit Christ, it means I desire Him to become a part of the spiritual home there. I am also admitting all the godly qualities which are a part of Jesus and must, in turn, become a part of me. I cannot open the door just a bit and allow only a small portion of Him to enter. It has to be cast wide open and with a cheerful, grateful embrace, welcome Him into my heart.

A warning here is necessary. The heart has no back door as far as Christ is concerned. Many people want to ask Him to go around and slip in unnoticed by their friends and neighbors. He will not do this for an important part of opening the door is the pride in letting all around us know Who has come to stay with us.

THE ENTRANCE HALL. I only mention this part of the heart home in a small way because Christ will go through here on His way into the other rooms of my heart. His passage is not the important part about this small area. It is brought into the lesson because too many Christians do not want Jesus to pass beyond this point. They feel He should be perfectly satisfied with this cramped space. He will not long remain if this is the only part we let Him share. So make certain we allow Him to come all the way into the home we ask Him to dwell in.

LIVING ROOM. As we pass together into this room, I will be saying to Christ, "Lord, I want this heart of mine to be yours. Make it your home. Everything I possess is now yours and from this time on we will live together in fellowship and harmony." We are now in the living room of my heart and we stop to look around. This is perhaps the most important room in all my life because the true influence of Christianity will be shown here to all around me.

Inviting Christ into this room carries with it the privilege and responsibility to fit every daily act into a pattern set for me by God's word. I will always be on the alert to show a pure, helpful, kind way of life to all I meet. There will never be any activity permitted here which Christ cannot wholeheartedly endorse. I may have to do some housecleaning, ridding my living room of unwholesome furnishing and decoration, but this will not grieve me. For Christ will make anything I have to give up seem as worthless as it really is. And like Paul, I can say, "To live is Christ."

KITCHEN. I include this room in home because as a woman it is my workshop, where I spend so much of my time. (I am not using the actual physical work of a kitchen in this comparison but simply the part that the work plays in my life.) I must surely see that Christ has a place in this room for unless He guides and directs and assists in all that I do, my work will be useless. To allow Him to enter my work area, means that He will be right beside me in every endeavor I undertake in this new life, whether it be in the homey task of preparing meals for my family or developing some talent to be used in the work of the church.

I may be unskilled and clumsy but with Christ as my Helper, I can have the same assurance as though He placed His hands on mine and guided them through the routine of the work before me. This realization helps me know that within myself I am nothing, but I can at the same time be extremely confident because my sufficiency is of Christ. His Spirit working with mine is as certain as the picture of His hands taking hold of mine to perform some task. He will be able to accomplish great things with my hands if I do not fight against His guidance but allow the free movement of His Spirit within me working His will and pleasure in all things.

DINING ROOM. This is my room of appetites and desires. It is almost certain that I will have to change the menu served previously because it tended to rely on "old bones, corn husks, sour cabbage, leeks, onions and garlic right out of Egypt." These were the things I liked — the worldly fare which I remembered from my past life. Now as a Christian and with Christ in my heart, my taste must change. I will desire that which is more gentle and spiritual — true food that will satisfy the appetite and nourish the body. Christ compared doing the will of His Father to the meat for His diet (John 4:32). And there is other food also — the bread of life, fruits of the spirit, and the living water. A diet of this kind will produce an entirely new appetite. I will no longer crave the lusts of the flesh but will partake of only those spiritual desires which will keep me safe and healthy.

STUDY and LIBRARY. This room is very important in my Christian life for here is where I seek solitude to refill my intellect and rebuild my physical stamina through rest and quiet. There are books on the shelves along the wall and I must be careful to discard those which no longer fit into my study pattern since Christ will be using this room now also. In fact we will probably have a closer relationship in this room than in any other. Here we will pray together and seek the throne of the Father in thanksgiving, honor and praise. Here I will study to know both the Father and the Son better and the materials I use will be those of high moral quality — no trashy literature will be found here.

Since this room will probably be used by Christ more than the others, I will want to spend much time here myself. I cannot leave my guest alone for long periods. He will not feel the need as much as I but He will miss me when I fail to meet Him in quiet study and meditation.

BEDROOM. I must allow Christ into this area of my heart also because this room shares the closest human relationship I have. If Jesus is allowed to guide and influence my role as a wife, my husband will surely think of me as a "worthy woman." Being a godly wife will help me to be more Christian in every other way also.

This room is also important because it is here that my physical body is clothed and prepared to face the world. I may have to clear the closet of some articles of clothing not suitable for a Christian. Now that Christ lives in this room also, I will be more modest in choosing my apparel, in my make-up, and my general appearance.

NURSERY. Christ must certainly be invited into this room which houses the gifts of God which came from the union of my marriage. The precious children which will be with us for only a few short years must come to know the Savior as intimately as their parents do. Each will learn to depend upon Him for comfort and to seek His help in all their problems — large or small. I will probably see results of Christ being in the home more quickly in this room than any other for children are quick to imitate the good example set before them.

RECREATION ROOM. This room may have to be completely re-decorated before Christ will want to come in. My previous associates will not be suitable to introduce to Christ nor can I expect Him to participate in my former activities. But then my desires no longer run to the same excess so with His help, this will not be too difficult. This room is needful because of the very meaning of its name. The purpose of recreation is to build up or re-create. When I see this, I recognize that my new pleasures will be those things which will serve to build me up mentally and physically. How mistaken I was about the things I did before — they either tore me down or tried to destroy me altogether. The decor for this room will show joy, happiness, satisfaction and friendship. But now all these will be real, not cheap imitations.

LAUNDRY. Though this room is not large it does play an important part in my life. For in it I keep the clothing of the family fresh and clean. Since I am concerned with the spiritual rather than the physical, my heart's laundry is no less vital. Christ must be my constant partner whenever I work in this area for there is no cleansing agent in the spiritual realm other than His blood. I must seek to do the same. Here our spiritual clothing will be cleansed from the spotting of lasciviousness, idolatry, sorcery, enmities, strife, jealousies, wraths, factions, divisions, partyings, envyings and drunkenness (Galatians 5:19-21). They will come out sweet and fresh and show themselves to be love, joy, peace, long-suffering, kindness, goodness, faithfulness, meekness and self-control. With Christ and me at work in the laundry room, we cannot help but be clothed in pure and righteous apparel.

HALL CLOSET. I am ashamed to let Jesus see this part of my heart's home and I will probably try to keep it locked away from Him. Here is where I keep all the petty things I grumble about; here is where I hide the secret desires I am ashamed to bring out in the open. This small area is packed with the things in my life which I do not want anyone to know about; the thoughts, lusts and deeds which I want to conceal. I have given Christ all the rest of my heart's home. Surely He will let me keep this tiny part for myself.

But the most important lesson I must learn is that Christ will not live with me under those circumstances. All must be open to Him; nothing must be hidden away to rot and contaminate the rest of the heart. He will not force me to open that closet, but He entreats with me to give Him the key. I may stall and stammer; I may demand my "rights." Still He asks entry into my most secret place! Finally I give the key to His care and turn to run and hide my shame because of what He will find there.

Before I can make a move, He has the door open and in a twinkling, all that was ugly and sinful before was gone! He had made the closet clean and like new in just the second I gave my will unto Him. I cannot help but feel better that all evil is gone from my life and to know that now Christ can live in every part of my heart.

Then I realized that what He did with that hall closet, He could do for my whole house. Here I had been keeping Him a guest in my home when what He yearned for was complete ownership! I had struggled to make each room acceptable for Him and even with my great effort, it would soon become dusty and cluttered again. He knew that if I gave my will unto Him, He could keep each room as fresh as that closet now was. I was no longer going to be a host in my heart; I was changing my position to servant.

My decision made, I gave the title deed to Christ and signed it over to Him. I knew this was not only for time, but eternity as well! "Here, Lord, is all that I am and have forever. You are the Lord and I will remain as the servant."

Do I regret my decision? Not for a moment for He knows how to keep it in shape and I am no longer torn apart with the problems and cares involved in living in my heart's home. Perfect peace is mine since Christ is Master of my heart. "For I know whom I have believed and am persuaded that he is able to keep that which I've committed to him against that day."

TO THINK UPON

1. At what time do you open your heart's door to Christ?

2. Will Christ be satisfied with being a "roomer" in your heart?

3. Can you think of other rooms in our heart where Christ must also live?

4. Discuss some of the "housecleaning" we must do before Christ will live in our heart.

5. What are some of the things we tend to keep hidden in our "hall closet?"

CHAPTER XIII

"THE HERITAGE I LEAVE"

Recently I read of a woman who willed $150,000 to her four cats. I also heard of a man who left his son three shoe boxes, a pair of glasses and a ball of twine. We can all agree that these are indeed strange inheritances. But the act of leaving something to others is not so strange or even unusual. Seldom do we pick up a newspaper without reading where some person has willed another certain wealth of property or valuable articles. Inheritances have become a normal part of our society. And yet, the world has become so materialistic in its thinking that we feel the thing we can leave to others is property, money or a precious object. We fail to realize that each person on earth leaves a heritage when they depart this life.

The word heritage means something left by one to another. The dictionary says it may or may not be money or some possession. Since by far the majority of us will not have great material wealth to leave, we should be busy preparing the heritage that everyone—regardless of possessions—can bequeath when they die.

Perhaps we do not like to think of this subject since it is, of necessity, connected with death. We should realize that not everyone is promised long years of preparation and for this reason, we should redeem every minute of what time we do have. Also, it is most often true, that those who wait until later years to prepare their heritage find that it has already been done in their early years—when they were too careless to pay much attention to it—and now it is almost too late to change it.

The most important fact is to face the knowledge that each of us is now storing up for the inheritance we will leave and we are doing this every single day of our life. Now, we may not be aware that we are doing it and for this reason we will be placing shabby, worthless things in our will. For the heritage we give to others will be the lessons they learn from the examples we leave. It will continue to be a steadfast support or else a detriment to them long after we are gone.

The Bible tells us how fleeting are our days—how short our lives! So we must be constantly alert in filling each day with that which will enrich both our own lives and the lives we come in contact with. Psalms 90:12 says "Teach us to number our days that we may apply our hearts unto wisdom." In other words, "Help us to realize how short a time we have here so that we may learn to put first things first."

The heritage we will be discussing is not the kind put in a written will or testament, nor will it be probated in a legal court. Rather, it will be written in the hearts and minds and lives of people who know us. If it is the proper kind of inheritance, guided by Christ and His principles, then it will far outlast any material possession we might give. In fact, its influence will be felt throughout all eternity!

As I said in the beginning, each person who has lived on earth leaves an inheritance—not only to their family, but also to their friends and casual acquaintances; their community and the world; and of great importance to Christians, to the church. What we leave is, of course, up to each individual. Our will can be filled with things of little value or perhaps no value at all—maybe even something that is harmful. Or our will can be overflowing with those blessings which can mean so very much to those who will inherit them. What we must remember is that each of us is making a will with our daily lives and we are responsible for making it contain the right things.

Because I will not be able to leave great material wealth when I depart, I must make a spiritual will. I thought perhaps by sharing what I would like to leave as a heritage, it might be of some help to you. Please notice that I said **would like to leave** for some of these things have not yet been placed in my will. I desire that they should be and am striving for just that in my life.

FIRST, TO MY HUSBAND. I want to leave the happiness of a full, rich life of Christian companionship. I want him to know that his love has been a shield of great strength to me—protecting me from my own foolishness in many instances. I want to leave him the pleasant memories of a well-kept house, good meals, interesting conversation and sympathetic understanding of his problems. Let him know that the gifts I appreciated most were not the material things but the great wealth of Christian character he was willing to give.

When he looks back, I want him to see the genuine peace and contentment which he helped bring to my life. Though the cares of keeping house, making the budget balance (and I was not always so good at that), and bringing up the children right seemed to press me with daily burdens, I hope that I shall leave him the thought that my life was made complete by sharing it with him. I pray that he might remember me first of all as a steadfast Christian and then second, as a cheerful, contented helpmeet who was truly suitable for his needs.

TO MY CHILDREN. I hope that my girls will be fully aware of the great love and concern I had for them—to know and understand that my actions were for what I felt was best, though they may not have been so pleasant for them. I want to leave them with the knowledge that I felt about them as David did when he wrote in Psalm 127:3, "Children are an heritage of God." For in sending them to their daddy and me, God knew the great blessings and happiness they would give us.

May they come to understand that I wanted them to possess true beauty and that kind comes only from within. Their physical features were not the most important thing to me, but those rare qualities of inner happiness and loveliness were what I was striving to help them acquire.

I hope they may remember me as good, kind and understanding— not the strict taskmaster I must have seemed to them at times. May they come to realize that a permissive love is not a true love. I want them to have the knowledge that recreation does not have to be questionable to be fun. May they remember that I tried to provide them with entertainment they could enjoy as Christians.

I want them to recognize the providence of God in their lives and be grateful and obedient because of His wonderful love for us. My desire is for them to see the great comfort and enjoyment that comes from reading and studying God's word and making it live in daily actions. I want them to remember prayer as a basic part of our family life. For above all, I want to leave them with a grand love for Christ and what He has done for our family. They will then be able to suffer the pain and sorrows of life with a deep trust that "all things fit together in a pattern for good to those that love the Lord."

Let them recall that I accepted each of them as a separate individual and tried, to the best of my ability, to fill their unique needs. May I have never violated a trust they placed in me. I would hope that I might live in such a way that each of my daughters could say, "I hope I am a mother just like you."

TO MY MOTHER. My father left me a tremendous spiritual heritage when he departed this world. Because he went before me, I cannot leave him anything except by passing along some of the good he gave me to those coming after. But I can leave my mother something. I can leave her with the knowledge that I was grateful for the part she had in making me what I am. I want her to know that without her help I could never have undertaken many of the opportunities for service which came to me. She was a keeper at home and in so doing, she freed me for countless areas of work which I could accept and perform in the knowledge that she made it possible. Therefore I leave her with the thought that any reward I might receive—earthly or divine—will be partly hers, for without her help and support, I could never have had the time from the less "glamorous" chores. I may not always have been the best daughter to her but she was the best mother she knew how to be.

TO ALL MY FAMILY. I have much to be grateful for in just being a part of so many wonderful people. I could not begin to mention each one nor the good they made a part of my life. But I do want to leave them the sure knowledge that all of us were blessed because we shared life together. I pray they will understand that much of the good I possess came because they loved me and helped me make my life better. To the special ones who taught me patience, faith, and who urged me on to higher levels of service, I will the blessing which can only come from knowing that you have done an appreciated job. May they remember about me only that which was kind, gentle and good. May their loving graciousness pass over all the imperfection and evil in me. And may we all someday be joined together without loss in a heavenly home to continue the love we possess for each other now.

TO MY FRIENDS. My life has abounded with the wonderful blessing of friends and I want to remember them in my will also. I hope they might have a more sympathetic concern for others by remembering my love for them and the great pleasure I received from sharing life with them. I want their lives to be richer and sweeter because of their association with me. I leave them with the knowledge that true friends are worth far more than earthly goods and without such, life would indeed be desolate. I hope they will have my testimony that gossip can do no good but can bring only harm. And may they never have heard me indulging in such a worthless pastime. I pray they will realize that God was our best friend and in looking back, may our every relationship seem better because of His influence.

TO MY CITY, MY NATION AND THE WORLD. Since I have little material wealth, it may seem strange when I say I want to leave my city, my nation and my world an inheritance. But it is possible to do just that and may God wake up each of us to this fact. I want to leave my community, America and the world the idea that life can be good—that citizens can live together in peace. I pray that my own actions proved that no matter what race, creed or color, I respected a person for what they could mean in my life. May I have done all possible to further the idea of the brotherhood of man.

I want my daily life to be such that every store clerk, every professional person and even everyone I meet on the street will be less irritated and more calm because of my influence—even if it is just a pleasant smile on my face. May I leave the knowledge that honesty is not an extinct virtue by my dealings in the business world. And that voting in each election is a privilege and a responsibility—one that is not engaged in without prayerful consideration of the issues and candidates in question.

I would live in such a way that the world can know that to God, all men are equally precious, that each soul is valuable and worth more than all the wealth in the world. May my relationship with every person I meet be based on the knowledge that I respect the good in them. While I do not like or condone the evil, I am not critical or condemning. I would leave the world the deep, abiding trust that comes only by depending upon God—with the realization that each person has the responsibility to develop what they are but also with the full understanding that without God, man is nothing.

I would hope that I might leave the world the desire to see only the good in others and to do all within its power to bring out that good and not cover it with evil. It is true that my heritage to the world seems insignificant when it stands alone, but just think, if every Christian would determine to leave that same heritage! It **would** change the world, it **would** be a leavening influence and power for good!

TO THE CHURCH. When I think of all that God has done for me through Christ, then I am certain that I want to leave something to the church. That may sound presumptuous—to think that a human can give anything to an institution founded by God. But stop just a moment and realize that it is only through the human part of the church that God's work is done today. We are His hands, His feet and His mouth. We are the instruments He uses. So to the human part of His church, I can leave something.

I would leave, first of all, the desire and ability to work and worship together in peace—and that love and understanding of one another must be a basic principle in doing this. For if the church cannot live in peace, how can it be a positive influence for Christ? I will leave faithfulness—both in attendance and in working at anything that comes to my hand. I would leave respect and obedience of the elders to all those in the church—accepting the fact that what these men decide might not be what I desired but that it was for the best of all.

I would leave the knowledge that each member must take up his individual responsibility—not cast it on others—and each should recognize and develop the abilities they possess. May they, by my own example, see the necessity and value of accepting their duty to be an evangelist for Christ. I would leave the realization that the gospel is truly good news and that others who have not heard must hear before it is too late.

I want to state again that I certainly have not perfected what I want to leave in my will. What I have shared with you is what I **desire** to leave and what I hope I am working at every day. Only when my will is "probated" and my heritage given to those listed will I know whether I have been successful. I would pray that the things mentioned will be what I leave and with God's help, I feel it can be.

In Psalm 16:6 David wrote that life had been good to him and that through God he had a goodly heritage. So if I can leave the heritage I desire to, it will be because God has made my life good and has aided me to have a "goodly heritage." Solomon was given great wisdom by God and it was in this wisdom that he advised "I will walk in the way of righteousness, in the midst of the paths of judgment that I may cause those that love me to inherit substance" (Proverbs 8:20, 21). It might have been that Solomon was thinking of material substance, but there is a lesson for us. If we want to be able to leave much to others in the way of spiritual blessings, we must do as Solomon—walk in the way of righteousness.

May we all realize that the church is God's heritage to us (Ephesians 1:11 and I Peter 5:3). He gave it to Christ and through Christ, we have obtained this inheritance. We can be joint heirs with Christ of all that belongs to God—and we know that everything belongs to Him. So we have both an inheritance to enjoy here on earth and one in heaven of unimaginable wealth and glory.

Just as we would not wish our heritage to others to go unheeded and unappreciated, may we never be guilty of such an attitude toward that which God, through Christ, has given us. May we take full advantage of the privileges and responsibilities of our inheritance so that when our time comes to depart this life, we may leave a true Christian heritage to all those who come after us.

TO THINK UPON

1. Why is a spiritual will so much more important than a material one?

2. What are some of the heritages you desire to leave your own family? your own community? your own congregation?

3. How can the heritage of just one person help the world?

4. What would "total commitment" have to do with preparing a spiritual will?

5. Can you think of a spiritual heritage left you by some dear friend or a member of your family?

Epilogue

So, dear friends, this little book has come to a close. I cannot gauge its value to you but I do know that it has made my life better just for the writing of it. Do you think I praise my work? Not at all. This is a way I have found to serve God and if by putting my thoughts and study on paper, I can help even one other person, my efforts have been worthwhile.

I told you before that I do not claim originality for every thought in this book. My life is a composite of much I have gleaned from countless good people in many parts of our nation. Perhaps your own life has touched mine somewhere along this path. If so, I am grateful for the good you gave me and with God's help, I shall try to pass it to others.

This "life with wings"—so abundant, so free, so glorious—can be yours. All it takes is the courage to put God "to the test." Jehovah spoke through Malachi the prophet, challenging the Israelites to prove Him, put Him to the test. "Prove me now herewith, saith Jehovah of hosts, if I will not open you the windows of heaven, and pour you out a blessing, that there shall not be room to receive it" (Malachi 3:10).

I urge you to have faith in this life simply because God is able to make it a reality for you. "Now unto him that is able to do exceeding abundantly **above** all that we ask or think, according to the power that worketh in us" (Ephesians 3:20). That godly power can accomplish far beyond your fondest dreams. How can you not trust your life to Him, wait on Him and "mount with wings as an eagle?" what glory awaits you is unspeakably magnificent! The abundant life in the midst of a world torn asunder with doubt and evil. Do you want to have this life? Don't be afraid; reach out your hand and take the hand of God. Submit your will to His and see—just see—if His promises are true; Won't you have the faith now to try your wings?

Parting Thoughts

This year a great American statesman passed from this life. He was not perfect but he did give his life to preserving the ideals of his country and making the world a better place. He traveled all over, viewing the good and the evil of mankind. Nevertheless he still saw that world as a pretty wonderful place. Adlai Stevenson was realistic and yet still optimistic. May I share some of his last words with you?

"Go placidly amid the noise and the haste and learn what peace there may be in silence. Speak your truth quietly and clearly; and listen to others, even the dull and ignorant; they too have their story. If you compare yourself with others you may become vain or bitter; for always there will be greater and lesser persons than yourself.

"Be yourself. Especially do not feign affection. Neither be cynical about love; for in the face of all aridity and disenchantment, it is as perennial as the grass. Take kindly counsel of the years, gracefully surrendering the things of youth. Nurture strength of spirit to shield you in sudden misfortunes. But do not distress yourself with imaginings. Many fears are born of fatigue and loneliness.

"Be gentle with yourself. You are a child of the universe no less than the trees and the stars. You have a right to be here. And whether or not it is clear to you, no doubt the universe is unfolding as it should.

"Therefore be at peace with God. And whatever your labors and aspirations in the noisy confusion of life, keep peace with your soul. With all its sham, drudgery and broken dreams, it is still a beautiful world."

May God bless you and help you to live the abundant life so that you, too, might know it truly is a good world because God is in it with you!

—Marge Green